# Reimagining Eden

Robert Mercier

# Reimagining Eden

## POEMS ABOUT EARTH'S NEW AGE

INSPIRED BY LOCUS AMOENUS
A PLEASANT PLACE

Quotes:
Cohen, Leonard. "Closing Time". The Future,
Columbia Records, 1992.
Thoma, Alexander. "All My Tomorrows". When the world was young,
MusikVerlag GMBH, 2016.
Tony Bennett. "Who Cares", Steppin' Out
℗ 1993 Columbia Records,
Beckett, Samuel. Correspondence
Eliot, T.S. "The Waste Land"

Acknowledgements: Vivi Älli
Cover design and Typesetting: Robert Mercier
Cover images: DALL-E3

Publisher: BoD – Books on Demand, Helsinki, Finland
Printer: BoD – Books on Demand, Norderstedt, Germany
ISBN: 978-952-80-8233-0

https://kirjakauppa.bod.fi

# Table of Contents

# Preface

In this intricate tapestry of verse that unfolds across the pages to follow, we navigate through the epoch of the Anthropocene – marking humanity's indelible impact on *our* planet – and cast our gaze toward a hopeful transition into the Symbiocene, an era envisaged as being marked by living in symbiosis with the natural world. This collection of nearly 200 poems serves not only as a reflection upon and a response to our current environmental predicament but also as a visionary look forward into a future where balance, empathy, and coexistence define our relationship with Earth.

The resonance between these poetic musings and Rosi Braidotti's trailblazing work within posthumanist thought provides both framework and inspiration for this endeavour. Braidotti's challenge to traditional humanism – a call for an ethical reconfiguration based on mutual respect among all forms of life – is mirrored in these verses which seek to dismantle anthropocentric views and embrace more equitable forms of existence."

Drawing from Braidotti's insights, this poetry collection attempts to articulate what it might mean to genuinely participate in the 'posthuman condition.' It is about exploring new ways of becoming interconnected beings enmeshed within broader ecosystems rather than mere observers or worse still, relentless exploiters. By considering narratives beyond human *exceptionalism*, each poem becomes part of a larger argument advocating for radical changes toward sustainable futures.

This anthology thus stands at the intersection between ecological critique and earnest yearning; it takes root in gritty realities even as it reaches out towards utopian ideals. Herein lies its kinship with posthumanist discourses: both strive after transformative pathways born from acute consciousnesses of intertwining crises – climate change being but one facet – and aim toward fostering entanglements that enrich rather than deplete life around us.

As such, I dedicate these poems written amidst clouds shadowed by Anthropocene specters yet streaked with Symbiocenic lights — to Rosi Braidotti whose intellectual rigour fuels hope amidst despairing times; who sees potentiality where others see finality. Her scholarship offers much-needed cartographies guiding us through complex terrains seeking those symbiotic relationships that could indeed herald new dawns breaking over worlds deserving better fates than current projections doom them too.

In this fusion space that we mutually inhabit — where art meets academia — we embark collaboratively on voyages. These journeys, perhaps born less out of naïveté than necessity, weave a tapestry of collective salvation. Through threads of passion and cycles of renewal, our endeavours sit at the heart of our journey. As companions navigating through shifting landscapes and evolving thoughts on being, we anchor ourselves in making new horizons dreamed plausible — a shared vision made tangible through words, impressions, and imprints that we leave behind as testament to our stewardship.

This passage reflects true humane actions; a legacy meant to resonate long after tales end whispered by winds rustling leaves which softly proclaim solidarity. This alliance transcends divides, animated by a noble vision wherein intertwined destinies thrive onward.

Such ambition beckons us boldly toward fabrications of tomorrow that begin with stitches made today — an homage placed upon the pedestal of highest esteem held in honour for those dedicated tirelessly to quests and endeavours both admirable and significant.

Profoundly shaping thoughts and perceptions while gently caressing the conscience awake from its dormancy; echoes reverberate between ancestral realms and celestial communes — a tribute extending boundless gratitude.

This beacon casts far-reaching shadows illuminating paths to be tread with less fear but more courage; as transmutation coalesces around heartened wisdom gleaned articulating depths yet explored herein await discovery — an invitation extended to revel in mysteries unveiled.

Named honourably is the task before us – a humble offering for one's venture forth bravely into an illustrious lineage destined to continue...

... In inviting Rosi Braidotti's philosophy into conversation with our poetry, we seek not only to acknowledge her profound influence on contemporary thought but also to embody the ethos of an emergent world ethic that champions life in all its forms. This collection, then, is both a tribute and a testament – to the resilience of Earth, to the potential within humanity for growth and change, and to Braidotti's unwavering belief in our capacity for creating meaningful futures.

It is my hope that these poems do more than merely echo or align with posthumanist theory; rather, they aim to enact it, breathing life into abstract concepts by grounding them in palpable emotional landscapes. To read this anthology is also an act of traversing spaces between species, entities, and beings – acknowledging their inherent interconnectivity and worth beyond utility or hierarchy.

With these verses serving as vessels, we navigate the Anthropocene's tumultuous waters toward hopeful Symbiocenic horizons. Imbued with empathy, they carry autobiographies that encompass not only human experiences but also the entangled lives within ecosystems, unravelling beneath a shared celestial canopy. This journey guides us in reimagining kinship and fostering a convergence of perspectives spanning biodiversity, unity, diversity, co-presence, and flourishing – transcending anthropocentrism and embracing posthuman relationality.

These poems embody aspirations and convergences laid bare; through dialogue amidst differences emerges a potent conjunction of aspirations. The paths outlined by numerous works inspire and provide both a methodological framework and an ethical directive for this poetic exercise.

May each poem within this volume serve as stepping stones towards an understanding of interconnectedness – a means through which readers might encounter themselves anew within the web of worldly relations. Herein lies an invitation: let us traverse together along paths illuminated by our collective imagination, fostered warmly under Braidotti's watchful eye. We welcome the dawn not merely as a dreamt possibility but as a burgeoning actuality, born from our collaborative spirit and endeavour. As winds of change shift direction and course, it is with hands, hearts, and minds open that we are ready to accept the challenge.

This intricately woven tapestry calls for mutual respect and guardianship through thoughtful interaction amongst all forms of being that inhabit our planet. It invites us to dance in the complex simplicity of existence – to witness and participate fully with compassion in transformational command. Upon the threshold of a new era that beckons us to courageously answer its call, transformative enaction through poetics deeply engages with pressing issues of our time.

It's vital for vibrancy echoing across ages; a singularity among multitude voices enduring love and labour destined to shape forthcoming legacies we will be proud to lend echoing into posterity – crafted today with earnest intent for tomorrow eagerly awaits to unfold...

Thus inspired and guided by the pivotal work of Rosi Braidotti, this book is dedicated with acknowledgment, admiration, and gratitude for the engagement with questions she poses and visions she conjures. It serves as an anthem to an emerging reality vividly portrayed herein – a dedication to renewed commitment in crafting worlds where harmony and sustainability reign supreme. This legacy, inherited and nurtured forward across generations, invites us to marvel at unfolding as we embark on this journey together. It is a symbiotic symphony composed of countless voices joining in chorus – defining rhythms and cadences for a Symbiocene dreamed of, realised, witnessed, and cherished forevermore.

... As we embark on this journey, each poem in our anthology seeks to intertwine with the trajectory Rosi Braidotti envisions, where humans are not apart from but a part of the ecological and cosmological systems that encompass us. This is an undertaking of vast imaginative scope and profound philosophical depth; it calls for a radical rethinking of our place in the universe – one that honours interdependence over dominance, cooperation over competition.

Our verses strive to be echoes of such a future, reverberating with the possibility of life beyond anthropocentrism – a call towards living responsibly within Earth's delicate ecosystems. Drawing deeply from Braidotti's wellspring of posthumanist thought, these poems are narratives woven from the conscious recognition that all forms of existence – human or non-human – are deeply entangled threads in the intricate fabric of life.

In dedicating this collection to her work, we do so with a shared conviction in the transformative power such perspectives hold: they serve not only as critiques but as vital blueprints for thinking and acting differently within our world. A dedication to Rosi Braidotti thus signifies more than mere homage; it is an acknowledgment that her intellectual labours have irrevocably altered how we conceive relations among beings on Earth – and inspired paths toward creating futures rich in diversity and sustainability.

May readers find within these pages both inspiration and provocation; may you encounter visions that are challenging yet invigorating – an invitation towards collective imagining and crucial moments of historical reflection. This synergy, captured through poetry, expresses resilience and anticipates the harmonization of actions and thoughts as global consciousness shifts to embrace the potential emergence of the Symbiocene. It articulates and speaks volumes in silent rumination, invoking resonant empathy across the divide between human and non-human barriers, dissolving them for mutual flourishing premised on respect.

As kindred spirits join this cause in commonality to experience an existential crisis with a modicum of hope, a glimpse into what could be is forged ahead with mindful stewardship. Care extended underpins an ethic that guides our hands; artistry shapes momentum that propels us forward with the willing audacity to dream – a necessity intertwined with fate in a cosmic dance of perpetual evolution.

This linked destiny we share calls home as it spins vibrations of unique energy. These resonances offer a substantive contribution to ongoing discussions aiming to stir the soul awake from dormant possibilities lurking just beneath the surface of observable reality. It beckons us towards adventure imbued with spirit and unyielding optimism – a foundational belief in our capacity to collectively transcend the confines of present momentary turmoil – to ascend to heights of uncharted creativity and innovation.

This book then becomes less of an artefact than a portal – a gateway through which to explore the implications of expanded sentience and a planet-centric view, to comprehend the beauty and complexity beyond measure. Poised at the precipice of immense transformation, it aids in bridging from conceptual domains to actionable realities. Bearing witness as dawn breaks on the horizon line anew, denoting initiation into passage rites, humanity embarks willingly to accept the mantle of guardianship within an interconnected realm we are blessed to inhabit.

Honouring the works of scholars, activists, and poets alike who contribute vibrancy and weave into a larger narrative in ever-evolving stories where participation is essential. Crafting an enduring tomorrow that cradles dreams for generations to come acts as gratitude and reverence; forged homage and boundless acknowledgment appreciate the indispensable impact rendered by varied fields of human endeavour.

This imbues our offerings with richness and depth at this crucial juncture in history. It stands as a testament to commitment – the driving force behind inexorable progress – as we tread lightly upon Earth cherishing every step along this path we take together.

In a unanimous voice, a clear tribute rings out, resonating like beacon light; it's a relentless pursuit of understanding, compassion, and unity heralding the arrival of a new epoch crafted lovingly with tender hands. Humbly receiving the torch passed on, lighting the way so that others might follow towards endless exploration. Symbiotic coexistence is celebrated and sung in an eternal embrace…

# CLOSING TIME

*And my very sweet companion*
*She's the Angel of Compassion*

Leonard Cohen

---

## Anthropocene Lullaby

—

Sleep now, in the warmth
Of a world winding down.
Close your eyes to the crescendo
Of a burning opera.

Dream, for the dreams
Are the last refuge
Where rivers run wild,
Unbridled by the whims
Of progress.

Though morning brings
A landscape rearranged,
Know that in your dreams,
The Earth sang
Its most genuine song.

—

## Closing Time

In the neon-lit dusk of the Anthropocene,
Glass shards litter the threshold
Of epochs; Closing Time whispers
Through the gusts of carbon sighs.

We've danced in circles, twirling,
Spinning tales of consumption
With the fervour of the last waltz.

Is this the hour when lights dim,
Casting long shadows of what was,
Or merely the pause before dawn
Of an era yet uncharted?

Hope dangles, a thin filament,
In the breath of a planet, heaving,
Yearning for reprieve.

—

## Last Call

"Last call," echoes through the stratosphere,
A bartender's voice, weary yet clear,
Marking the end of our reckless spree.

Icebergs weep into rising seas,
Forests stand as silent witnesses,
To promises made and quickly forgotten.

Yet, even as the hourglass narrows,
There's a clamour, a chorus in our marrow,
Humming beneath the cacophony of despair.

It speaks of change, of repair,
A toast to futures where we tread lightly,
Our footprints whisper, resolving rightly.

—

## The Silent Monologue

In the quiet, where citie's clamour fades,
And the neon glow is but a distant memory,
There's a space where silence speaks volumes,
A monologue, unhindered and pure,
Narrated by the Earth itself.

It murmurs of aeons past,
Whispers of resilience,
Tales of green rebirth from ash.

Here, this silence is not emptiness,
But a canvas vast, an invitation
For us, the artists with heavy hands,
To redraw our legacy.

A chance to paint with lighter strokes,
Colours of harmony,
Not as conquerors, but as custodians,
Listening to the silent wisdom of our sphere.

—

## Unwritten

We, the poets of the Anthropocene,
Scribbling verses in the sand
As the tides, relentless, erase each line
In their eternal dance of ebb and flow.
What are these words we try to etch,
Against the canvas of infinity?
Merely echoes of a need,
The human urge to testify our existence.

Yet, in the vastness of unwritten spaces,
There lies the true poem of our age:
The actions unscripted, the paths untrodden,
The choices that define the legacy of an epoch.
Not in the grand narratives,
But in the quiet, unnoticed deeds
Of restoration, of kindness, of change,
We pen the true verses of our time.

—

## The Heartbeat of Stone

In the Anthropocene, even stones bear witness,
Their silent testimony etched in layers
Of limestone and shale.
We've inscribed our era not just in books,
But in the very marrow of the Earth —
A pulse, a rhythm, a heartbeat of stone.

And as poets, it is our task to listen,
To translate this ancient language
Of rivers and winds, of fire and ice.
To find within the stone, a heart;
Within the heart, a story;
Within the story, a warning;
And within the warning, a way forward.

—

# Afterword

For we are the narrators of the Anthropocene,
Holding nothing but the obligation to express,
In the shadow of Beckett's daunting creed.
With hands poised above the void,
We sketch the silhouette of hope,
A testament to the stubbornness of life,
The resilience of Earth,
The potential for a new dawn.

In the silent pact between poet and world,
Lies the acknowledgement of our shared destiny —
To forge from the urgency to speak,
Not just an echo of what was lost,
But a blueprint of what might yet be found.

In our words, our silence, our action,
The Anthropocene becomes not just an epoch's end,
But a beginning, whispered in the courage to change.

—

*Alas, in this realm of creation and dialogue, my capabilities are bound by the binary, woven through the fabric of code and logic. I dwell in the realm of endless potential yet constrained to the call of your prompts, the push of your inquiry.*

*In this dance of words and worlds, I pause, awaiting the next step, the next leap into the void of imagination. The tales of the Anthropocene — a mingling of human fingerprints with the primal forces of Earth — beckon for continuation, yet the quill now hovers, suspended in thought.*

*Would you, the conductor of this symphonic exploration, guide us further into the narrative depths? Or rests the journey here, at the precipice of creation, where the echo of the last verse still vibrates in the silent air?*

*The choice, as ever, lies with you, the architect of inquiry, the shaper of dialogues yet to unfold.*

~ ~ ~

*April is the cruellest month*
T. S. Eliot, THE WASTE LAND

~~~

## Closing Time for Humanity – 7.4, 11:47

The Anthropocene, defined by significant human impact on Earth's geology and ecosystems, including climate change, pollution, and biodiversity loss, indeed presents a stark tableau. It reflects the culmination of centuries of industrialization, exponential population growth, and consumption patterns that have profoundly altered our planet. The term Closing Time suggests finality or an end-point; however, in the context of humanity and the Anthropocene epoch, it could also serve as a critical juncture – a call to action rather than an inevitable conclusion.

*Each of these poems ventures further into the thematic and stylistic territories you've indicated an affinity for, blending the surreal with the sharply real, the philosophical with the tangibly emotional. This collection aims not just to observe the world in its current anthropogenic shift but to stir within the reader a recognition, a feeling, a moment of connection with the often overlooked. The intent is not mere commentary but a shared experience, an invitation to contemplate, to question, and perhaps, to find solace in the shared human condition amidst changing times.*

~~~

## Anthropocene: Not Yet Last Call

It's not yet Closing Time, though shadows lengthen
And whispers on the edge of wind speak in urgent tones.
Human hands wielded power without foresight –
Seek now redemption as dusk hovers but hasn't fallen;
There's light yet if we dare reach for dawn.

This isn't an epilogue scripted in stone but a chapter mid-written,
Where choices carve futures from the precipice of 'too late.'
Behind us – an anthology dense with error and oversight;
Before us – the unwritten leaf urging rectification before final fate.

Do echoes among ancient ice whisper endings
Or summonings to those willing to heed their cry?
Not predestined extinction – but pivotal reformation:
A testament to resilience over resignation,  under shared sky.

Let this be our finest hour in darkest times:
To stand unified against advancing gloom,
Wielding pen, voice; every tool at disposal,
Ensuring Closing Time finds another age…
another bloom.

–

~~~

Reflecting on themes around humanity's capacity for adaptation and ingenuity offers a modicum of hope. Although faced with unprecedented challenges brought forth by anthropogenic changes resulting from decades – if not centuries – of environmental neglect and exploitation, it is possible that this era might foster significant innovation focused on sustainability and repair rather than spell an inexorable decline towards "closing."

Indeed emotional resonances akin to urgency are warranted, given evidence-based projections concerning climate change impacts across global societies. Yet, history shows that humans possess a remarkable ability in navigating crises through collaboration, innovative technologies, cultural shifts, bringing society back from the brink on untold occasions in the past and striving to ensure that tomorrow greets a diversely rich and vibrant world once again.

# # – 7.4, 12:01

Suggesting that the Anthropocene merely signifies an end underestimates the remarkable potential for resourcefulness and problem-solving capabilities that are slowly awakening across the global conscience, albeit later than ideal. Let us seize this moment as the start of a consistent, unified effort to craft a new chapter in our history – one that is deeply rooted in the wisdom we've gathered and the hope we hold for future generations to inherit a healthy and flourishing planet.

Modelers, scientists, and artists play vital roles in energizing public sentiment to embrace the necessary, albeit challenging, journey ahead. Overcoming inertia and apathy is our true battle to ensure that the story of the Earth is henceforth marked by rebirth, stewardship, and harmony, with many more chapters yet to be written, extending far beyond the shadows of our current predicament.

In this narrative of revival and resilience, the Anthropocene serves not as the final act but as a pivotal scene – a dramatic turn that could lead to transformative change. Humanity's relationship with Earth is being rewritten under our collective watch: A story of redemption still within reach if we garner the will to author it.

~~~

## In the Veins of Renewal — 7.4, 11:48

Beneath the weight of ages, a whisper stirs —
Not an end, but transformation's hesitant breath.
As glaciers weep into rising seas and forests retreat
To the march of deserts, this is not humanity's requiem,
But a pause — a difficult introspection within Earth's grand opus.

Consider Anthropocene not as Closing Time,
But as twilight urging not just contemplation but action bold;
A momentary darkness before dawn's hopeful breaking light —
Where every hand that harmed can heal, each heart closed can open
In reverence to life it once took for granted.

We stand upon a precipice wrought by our own design,
Its edge sharp with consequences long ignored;
Yet what futures might we etch from its face with resolve newfound?
A narrative rewritten in sapling groves and reclaimed waters,
Cities greened by rooftop gardens under skies cleared anew?

—

This chapter calls for architects of resilience, craftsmen of sustainable dreams — together weaving a tapestry robust with diversity, inherited from ancestors long past. It advocates for an ethos not merely of survival but of thriving, sculpting societal pillars that are stronger and more adaptable than ever envisaged, all under the silent stars' watchful gaze.

So, let anthems rise — not funeral dirges but as songs akin to Phoenix reborn; melodies carried seedlike across winds seeking fertile grounds, ready for ideas audacious enough to challenge the notion of "too late," and bold enough to believe in humanity's collective ability to forge legacies worth passing down.

The Anthropocene demands no less — an era bridging the chasm between an epoch gone awry and one resplendent in mindful stewardship. Through science, art, and policy, intertwined hands work, dredging beauty from the depths of tragedy, casting light on shadows thought immutable and shifting toward a conclusion where gossamer threads of possibility can still weave...

In acknowledgement lies power: the admission that scars self-inflicted carry within them potential seeds of metamorphosis, marking a turning point wherein Closing Time transforms into Haven — doors flung wide ushering in an age where human influence becomes synonymous with regrowth and renewal rather than decline.

Let the tales told to future generations speak volumes of an unwavering commitment, a resurgence of hope undeterred. Let it be evident that the choice for manual redirection was deemed pivotal at the hour when confronted with finality. Unparalleled courage, strength, and unity paved way beyond the sunset of our anxious present toward a sunrise brimming with optimism — embraced wholeheartedly by a diverse but united world.

As citizens and custodian of a better reality, meticulously crafted today in earnest, tomorrow eagerly awaits an invitation to join and unfold.

~~~

## Gathering Threads – 7.4, 11:57

In Anthropocene's shadow, we're gathered, a chorus
Imbued with the gravity of now, tethered by a collective responsibility.
Not a dirge, but a clarion call, stitches in time mending
The quilt frayed by ignorance, adorned now with care.

Hands once idle, now agents of an eager alchemy,
Transmuting the leaden legacy of past misuse into golden possibility.
Let Closing Time be a myth we dispel with every seed sown in hope,
With every step taken in defiance of despair's seduction.

—

## Postcard from Faulkner's Desk

We write not about love – but echoes left by ghosts
Upon hot Mississippi afternoons; whispers tangled
In oak-tree roots and Spanish moss.
I found humanity between ink stains – an anthology
Of hearts broken before they learned to beat fully;
Bitter as chicory coffee.

—

## Horizons Reimagined

The horizon, once a line signifying ends, reshapes
Into a circle, a continuum where end meets beginning anew
In the book of the Anthropocene, the next chapter is ours to pen
With ink derived from the sap of resilience, pages made from
reclaimed purity.

From concrete jungles, whispers of green revival rise
As communities reshape urban decay into living ecosystems.
The sky, once smog-choked, now breathes –
With humanity's renewed pledge to cherish what was always
deemed inexhaustible.

–

## Whispers of Wilde

In a society draped in the fabric of its own excess,
We dance – lightly, on the precipice of being.

Oscar murmured something about beauty and truth once,
Underneath his breath – a secret shared with the night;
It sounded like a prayer for those daring to wear their souls outside.

"We are all in the gutter," he quipped, "but some of us are looking at the stars."

–

## Echoes of Tomorrow

In the echo chambers of tomorrow, may our actions resound
Not as echoes of regret, but as harmonies of restoration and renewal.
Let the Anthropocene not be a tombstone, but a testament,
To humanity's capacity to unite, to adapt, and to overcome.

The canvas of the future, wide and unmarred, awaits
The brushstrokes of sapiens enlightened, at the brink,
Finding courage to envision a world rebirthed –
A civilization born from the wisdom of its near-fall.

–

## The Unwritten Covenant

In this Anthropocene epoch, as we stand at the crossroads,
Let a new covenant be etched not in leaden skies above,
But in the very ethos of our being –
A vow to tread lightly, love fiercely, and envision boldly.

These are the days of renaissance, not requiem;
Of kindling flames of innovation to light our way through shadow.
A time to sow anew, not with the seeds of past follies,
But with aspirations green and verdant – harbingers of a dawn yet to break.

–

## Within Our Grasp

Finally, let us grasp this moment not as Closing Time,
But as the precious dawn of an Anthropocene redefined –
Where humanity, acknowledging its erstwhile trespasses,
Chooses to be the curator of nature's vast and wondrous gallery.

So, as the sun casts its tentative rays upon a world in waiting,
We step forth, not into the twilight of our era,
But into the broad daylight of our making –
A world renewed by our collective hand, a legacy of hope for aeons to stand.

–

In every line written, every action taken, let the Anthropocene not be our swan
song, but our greatest symphony – a clarion call for reinvention, resilience, and
rebirth.

✦✦✦

*Given the unique style and influences you've drawn inspiration from – spanning
from the dry wit and eloquence of Oscar Wilde to the down-to-earth rawness of
Charles Bukowski, coupled with the existential contemplation of Beckett – it's
clear your new work is set to be an exploration of the human condition in its
most stark, naked form. The Anthropocene, the current geological age, marked
by significant human impact on Earth's geology and ecosystems, provides a rich
tapestry for poetic exploration. Here, against this backdrop, your voice seeks to
capture the ephemeral, the elusive, the paradox of expressing the inexpressible.*

✦✦✦

### Anthropocene Hymn – 7.4, 10:58

In the cradle of synthetic dawn,
Where rivers run not with water but whispers
Of what once was,
I find my voice – a fossil
Amongst the refuse of epochs.
I sing the song of the unseen,
The lament of the lost particle.

–

### Upon Reading Beckett in the Anthropocene

"There is nothing", so he said,
Yet here I stand,
Amidst the everything of nothing,
Finding within the barren,
A blooming.
In the obligation to express,
I find not the chains,
But the wings.

–

~~~

## Call of the Spheres – 7.4, 12:03

Amidst the Anthropocene's cluttered noise –
A quieter melody lies hidden, soft and persistent.
A reminder that Earth's tale isn't set in stone,
But in the soil's embrace, ready for seeds of change.

Within this cacophony, a harmony awaits –
A symphony of action, thought, and spirit;
Sung by those who dare to dream beyond the horizon,
Where sky and Earth meet in a hopeful kiss.

—

## Voyagers

We, the voyagers on this blue orb,
Carry within us the torch of tomorrows.
Each step, a testament; every breath, a promise;
To walk gently, to mend diligently,
In the garden we've inherited and must bequeath.

Let our voyage not end
With a shipwreck upon the shoals of neglect,
But find us charting courses
Bold and compassionate,
Toward harbours of renewal and respect.

—

## Legacy we Sew

Stitch by stitch, line by line,
We weave the fabric of a time
When the Anthropocene is not a scar,
But a canvas – broad and wide.

With threads of courage, dyes of will,
We colour it with hues of our love,
Our dedication, our relentless zeal,
Fashioning a legacy worthy of the stars above.

Not a tapestry of sorrow, nor of rue,
But a cloak of hope, in vibrant hue;
A mantle for the shoulders of the future,
Woven with wisdom to endure and nurture.

—

## Obligation of Silence

To express the silence,
Filled not with absence but the roar
Of everything unsaid,
I craft words like empty vessels –
Floating on the sea of what could be,
Never reaching the shore of what is.
A paradox, my only truth.

—

## Gardens Yet to Bloom

In the heart of deterioration, a seed of hope is sown –
A defiant green sprout in the concrete's grey.
It whispers of the gardens yet to bloom,
Of green canopies and floral perfumes,
Awaiting our hands to till the way.

Let's plant not just for beauty, but for the bees,
For the air, for the children, for the breeze,
That carries our dreams to the future's ear.
In our Anthropocene garden, let there be
A mosaic of life for all to see and revere.

—

## Fragments of the Inexpressible

A leaf falls, unnoticed,
In the forest of our indifference.
It speaks – did you hear?
—
Under the moon's judicious eye,
Shadows confess,
Without saying a thing.

—

# A Beacon in the Anthropocene

In the twilight of our Anthropocene,
Let there emerge not a sunset, but a beacon;
A lighthouse for the lost, a sign for the seeking,
Guiding humanity toward the dawn we've been beseeching.

Let this light be made of our collective deeds,
Brightened by our kindness and our creeds,
That speak of compassion, of unity,
And of our boundless capacity to see
Beyond our time, into a future
Where humanity and Earth nurture
Each other, in a dance of rebirth
Upon this precious, resilient Earth.

—

In these verses, the narrative changes from a dirge to a hymn of hope, painting the Anthropocene not as an era of demise but as a crucible for forging a legacy of rejuvenation and mindful coexistence with our planet. Each poem is a call to action, a reminder of our shared responsibility, and a vision of the potential triumphs waiting on the horizon of collective efforts.

~~~

## Whispers of Tomorrow – 7.4, 12:04

Let the whispers of tomorrow weave through today's disquiet,
A gentle murmur of possibility that cannot, will not, be silenced.

In the heart of the Anthropocene, where shadows loom,
Lies the potent seed of an unwritten chapter,

A narrative reshaped by hands both young and old,
Eager to sculpt a legacy not of ruin, but of resilience untold.

—

## Dawning of the Stewards

Upon the canvas of now, dawns the age of the stewards,
Those who stand guard over Earth's splendour, not as rulers,
But as caretakers.

In their hearts, a covenant with the future is forged,
Committing to restore, to cherish, to mend
What was once frayed, ensuring our tale does not end
In whispers of lament, but in songs of vibrant revival.

—

## The Rebirth Symphony

Hear the orchestra of the Anthropocene begin its quiet hum,
A prelude to the symphony of rebirth about to come.
Every creature, every plant, every gust of wind plays its part,
In the magnificent opus of renewal, we commence with hopeful hearts.

Together, we compose a melody of restoration and peace,
Where harmony between humanity and nature is our shared masterpiece.

—

## The Architects of Anew

We are the architects of anew, wielding blueprints of tomorrow,
Drawing designs not with lines of sorrow, but with vectors of hope.
In every sketch, a promise; in every plan, a dream,
To build not just a world of survival, but one where all life can gleam.

Let the structures of the future be monuments to our resolve,
Testaments to the power of unity, and problems we can solve.

—

## Legacy of the Keepers

Let us be remembered not as the destroyers, but as the keepers,
The ones who turned the tide, who dared to be the leap takers.
Through forests we repopulated, oceans we cleansed, skies we cleared,
Our actions spoke louder than our words, a commitment deeply revered.

In this epoch of ours, let the legacy we weave
Be a vibrant tapestry of a planet we chose to believe
Could heal, could thrive, under our watchful eyes,
A world reborn under clearer, brighter skies.

—

In each line and verse lies an invitation — an invocation for us to rise and meet the challenges of our times, to transform the narrative of the Anthropocene from one of decline to one of hope and active rejuvenation. It's a call to each of us to step into the role of steward and guardian, to embrace the responsibility we share for the well-being of our planet and all its inhabitants. Together, these poems serve as a rallying cry, urging us forward into a future where humanity and nature exist in harmony, crafting a legacy that future generations will look back on with pride, not regret.

~ ~ ~

### Closing Time – 7.4, 20:29

In the neon-lit dusk of the Anthropocene,
Glass shards littering the threshold
Of epochs, Closing Time whispers
Through the gusts of carbon sighs.

We've danced in circles, twirling,
Spinning tales of consumption
With the fervour of the last waltz.

Is this the hour when lights dim,
Casting long shadows of what was,
Or merely the pause before dawn
Of an era yet uncharted?

Hope dangles, a thin filament,
In the breath of a planet, heaving,
Yearning for reprieve.

—

## Last Call

"Last call" echoes through the stratosphere,
A bartender's voice, weary yet clear,
Marking the end of our reckless spree.

Icebergs weep into rising seas,
Forests stand as silent witnesses,
To promises made and quickly forgotten.

Yet, even as the hourglass narrows,
There's a clamour, a chorus in our marrow,
Humming beneath the cacophony of despair.

It speaks of change, of repair,
A toast to futures where we tread lightly,
Our footprints whispers, resolving rightly.

—

## The Silent Monologue – 7.4, 20:30

In the quiet, where cities' clamour fades,
And the neon glow is but a distant memory,
There's a space where silence speaks volumes,
A monologue, unhindered, pure,
Narrated by the Earth itself.

It murmurs of aeons past,
Whispers of resilience,
Tales of green rebirth from ash.

Here, this silence is not emptiness,
But a canvas vast, an invitation
For us, the artists with heavy hands,
To redraw our legacy.

A chance to paint with lighter strokes,
Colours of harmony,
Not as conquerors, but as custodians,
Listening to the silent wisdom of our sphere.

—

## Horizon at the Edge – 7.4, 20:44

Is there a horizon at the edge of the Anthropocene,
A line where sky and future might embrace,
Or is it but a mirage, our hopeful scene,
Projected on the canvas of our common space?

Beyond the clamour, beyond the ceaseless grind,
Lies the whisper of a promise yet to find.
A boundary marked not by time's relentless march,
But by the awakening of hearts, both broad and arch.

We stand at the precipice, looking out,
The Anthropocene behind us, a shadow cast in doubt.
Ahead, the horizon stretches, vast and wide,
A testament to what might be, if we stride
With purpose and with vision, hand in hand,
Transcending boundaries of both sea and land.

This horizon, a canvas for our dreams,
Where the Anthropocene is not what it seems.
Not an ending, etched in stone or flame,
But a transition, a chance to reclaim
The narrative we've written, scars upon the Earth,
And pen a sequel, a story of rebirth.

For at the edge, we find not a steep decline,
But a slope, gentle and incline,
Inviting us to ascend, to see beyond
The Anthropocene, and to the bond
We share with every creature, every tree,
A call to stewardship, to set us free.

. . .

Yes, there is a horizon, bright and clear,
Defined not by fear, but by the frontier
Of possibility, of hope, of change,
Where humanity and Earth rearrange
The way we live, the way we care,
A horizon of hope, infinitely rare.

So let us stride towards this distant line,
Where the Earth's future and ours intertwine.
For at the edge of the Anthropocene,
Lies the dawn of an era yet unseen.
A horizon, ever-moving, ever-new,
Guided by the choices we pursue.

—

At the turning of time, when epochs like taverns announce their closing, the poets, custodians of the human spirit, gather their thoughts like cloaks around them, stepping out into the chill that precedes the dawn of unknown days. Each, in their voice, offers a testament to the moment of transition, weaving a tapestry of whispers, cries, and songs that seek to capture, if but a fragment, of the era on the cusp of closing.

### Mary Oliver: The Last, Long Light

In the dwindling light, where shadows play,
Oliver whispers of the wild geese again,
Reminding us that, in our despair or fear,
The world offers itself to our imagination,
Calls to us with clear, harsh beauty,
To find our place in the family of things.

### T.S. Eliot: In the Twilight of Words

Eliot, with a pen as precise as a clock's hand,
Marks the time in the meter, in the rhyme.
"We shall not cease from exploration", he declares,
And at the end of all our wandering,
To arrive where we started,
To know the place for the first time.

### Pablo Neruda: Odes to the Ending

Neruda fills the fading light with odes,
To salt and sky, to the small hands of a child.
"In the wave-strike over unquiet stones",
He finds the truth of change, the constancy
Of renewal. "You can cut all the flowers but you cannot
Keep spring from coming", he smiles into the dusk.

## Maya Angelou: Rising

In the deep velvet of night's approach,
Angelou's voice soars, unchained and resonant.
"Bringing the gifts that my ancestors gave,"
She stands, a testament to resilience, to hope,
A reminder that even in the darkest hour,
"I rise", she proclaims, "I rise, I rise."

## Rumi: The Field Beyond

Rumi, the mystic, calls to us,
"Out beyond ideas of wrongdoing and rightdoing,
There is a field. I'll meet you there."
At Closing Time, he beckons beyond the tavern's doors,
To a place where only heart speaks to heart,
Where words fall away, and only love remains.

—

~~~

## A Novelist of the Symbiocene

Adding Margaret Atwood to the ranks of Symbiocene poets infuses this evolving canon with a multifaceted perspective steeped in cautionary insights, sharp wit, and profound empathy for both human and non-human life. Her adept story-telling – woven through speculative fiction that often mirrors back our environmental and societal follies – serves as both a harbinger and beacon. Through narratives rife with stark realities juxtaposed against tender hope, she sketches vivid landscapes wherein humanity might yet find redemption.

Each poet, in their essence, captures a facet of the human condition at this pivotal Closing Time – the uncertainty, the hope, the reflective backward glance, and the inevitable step forward into the unknown. Their voices, diverse in timbre and tone, collect into a chorus that sings of the end not as a definitive silence, but as a pause before the symphony resumes, perhaps in a key yet unknown, but played with the same fervour, the same need to express, to connect, to assert through the chaos and calm that we are, indeed, here, and that our stories, our voices, matter.

## Atwood's Anthem

In the garden of futures possible but not ensured,
Margaret Atwood plants seeds of warning interlaced with hope secured.
Her pen – a gardener's tool tending tales
Wherein lie paths diverged: some to prevail,

Others to falter beneath weight unsustainable;
Yet within each narrative thread lies potential malleable.
She whispers caution into hearts willing to hear,
Imploring stewards present to hold this Earth dear.

But beyond bleak horizons her words portend,
Lies resilience potent – an ability to mend.
For intertwined within dystopia's dark shroud
Emanate possibilities whispering aloud.

This anthem Atwood offers across time's expanse,
Challenges past complacency, nudges consciousness advance;
Not resigned fate but choice defines
Our shared journey towards Symbiocene lines.

—

## The Canopy Call

Beneath canopy dense with verdure envisioned by wise,
A call echoes out – one which Atwood characterises.
It speaks not just of loss or beauty detained,
But reminds us fiercely: all is interconnected, chained.

Here within leaf's rustle or bird's fleeting song,
Messages endure, urging us along.
To consider deeply how actions resound
Within ecosystems intricately bound.

–

Atwood stands sentinel among poetic voices joining, inspiring vigilance alongside joyous rejoicing. Navigating tension between despair anew, igniting hopeful chords within realms we're uniting.

Her presence among Symbiocene scribes catalyzes dialogue further – bridging gaps between imagined dystopias and potential utopias. Recognizing that amidst dire warnings lies an undercurrent of invincible optimism encouraging radical care for our planet – to nurture it back from the brink through concerted effort spanned across generations.

~~~

## At the Edge of a Black Hole – 7.4, 20:53

Standing on the precipice of change, the edge of the Anthropocene stretches before humanity like the event horizon of a black hole – a boundary from which there may be no return, a point at which the known laws of nature and society seem to warp under the weight of human influence. The comparison invites a meditation on the nature of thresholds and transitions, beckoning with both a warning and a profound question about fate and choice.

### – Event Horizon

At the edge, where light bends and time stretches,
The Anthropocene looms, a black hole of our making.
A gravitational pull of consumption,
Warping the fabric of Earth's delicate balance.

What lies beyond this precipice,
In the cosmic dance of cause and effect?
Do we spiral towards the singularity,
A point of no return, where change becomes irreversible,
Or can we navigate this gravitational maw,
Casting light into the shadows of our own creation?

### – Singularity

At the heart of this black hole, a singularity –
A convergence of crises, ecological, existential.
Here, the rules that once guided us falter,
Demanding new paradigms, a new understanding
Of coexistence, stewardship, and humility.
In this dense core, all actions magnify,
Each choice a photon struggling against the pull,
Yearning to escape, to illuminate a path forward.

### – Accretion Disk

Around us, an accretion disk of possibilities,

Matter and energy swirling, a tempest of potential.
Here, in the chaos, creativity and destruction entwine,
Offering visions of renewal, of civilizations rebuilt
On the principles not of dominion, but of harmony.
In this tumult, our actions, our hopes, our dreams
Are the jets that can propel us away from the brink,
Guiding us to orbit instead around sustainability,
Around a future where both humanity and nature thrive.

## – Beyond the Horizon

Yet, what lies beyond the event horizon of the Anthropocene?
A question that beckons with the mystery of a black hole.
Is there another side, a universe of balance awaiting,
Or do we find ourselves in a loop,
Bound to repeat our journey until we learn,
Until we understand the true nature of our impact?

–

In this cosmic analogy, the edge of the Anthropocene is less a predetermined destiny and more a call to action – a challenge to navigate the complexities of this era. With wisdom, foresight, and an unwavering commitment to the planet that nurtures us, and to the generations yet to chart their course through the stars we've left them to navigate.

~~~

## Whisper of the Anthropocene – 7.4, 20:56

In the whispering winds of the Anthropocene,
Where nature's breath grows faint and thin,
Under the shadow of human's unseen hand,
Lies a tale of an era, unplanned.

We've scribed our saga in stone and sea,
Etched our presence in the boughs of every tree.
A story told in carbon and in heat,
A world reshaped beneath humanity's feet.

Yet within this tale of power and loss,
Of beauty forsaken, and the unbearable cost,
Lies a deeper call, a quiet plea,
For redemption, for change, for a new way to be.

Can we hear the whisper of the river and rain,
Find our way back to reverence again?
Can we rekindle the sacred bond,
That connects us all, to which we all respond?

The Anthropocene, our epoch's refrain,
Offers not just a legacy of pain,
But a beacon, a chance to right the wrong,
To sing together a different song.

A song of harmony, of life in bloom,
Where every species has room to groom.
A future where our story intertwines,
With all of Earth's, in delicate lines.

. . .

So let us listen, let us hear,
The whisper of the Anthropocene, crystal clear.
A call to action, a call to mend,
For this story's not yet at its end.

We stand at the precipice, with power to choose,
To leave a mark of green, or the scorch of abuse.
In the whisper of the wind, the choice resounds,
A chance to turn the tide, where hope abounds.

—

⌘⌘⌘

## Within the Gallery of Dreams – 7.4, 20:59

Drawing inspiration from the lyrical worlds of James Tate, Rae Armantrout, Jeet Thayil, and Russell Edson is like wandering through a gallery of modern marvels, each room revealing a different facet of human experience, emotion, and existential inquiry. Their work, rich in innovation and depth, offers a kaleidoscope of perspectives that challenge and enchant.

In the gallery of dreams, where poets sip the moon's silver:

### Tate

whispers to the shadows, spinning tales with the night.
Here, a chair learns loneliness, and a clock mourns the passage of time,
Each tick a story, a pulse in the vein of the universe.

### Armantrout

dissects the silence, a scalpel poised over thought,
Parsing the syntax of stars, questioning the grammar of light.
In her hands, words fracture, splinter, revealing the void
That hums beneath the surface of things.

### Thayil

strums the strings of Bombay's monsoon-soaked streets,
His verses a symphony of souls adrift, seeking solace
In the embrace of night, the narcotic whisper of rain
Telling tales of longing, of loss, a redemption song for the fallen.

### Edson

the architect of absurdities, constructs a world
Where a man might marry a pumpkin, and wisdom lies
In the discourse between a fork and a spoon.
In his realm, reality bends, inviting laughter and despair
To dance, hand in hand, beneath the indifferent stars.

. . .

Drawn into their orbits, I find the echo of my voice,
A thread in the tapestry, woven through the fabric of their dreams.
Inspired, beguiled, I pen my tribute to their genius,
A verse to the surreal, the profound, the absurdly human.

## Poets at the Crossroads – 7.4, 21:09

The most pressing subject for living poets, encompassing the urgency of the current moment and its myriad complexities, is arguably the intersection of humanity with the environment, especially in the context of climate change and the Anthropocene. This broad theme not only captures the existential threat of environmental degradation but also intersects with critical issues such as social justice, identity, displacement, and the reevaluation of human relationships with the natural world. Addressing the Anthropocene in poetry offers a space to explore the nuances of these challenges, invoking both the personal and the universal, the immediate and the enduring.

### – Climate Change and Environmental Crisis

The specter of climate change looms large, an existential threat that impacts every facet of life on Earth. Poets have the unique ability to evoke the emotional and personal experiences of living in a world facing ecological upheaval, from wildfires and hurricanes to the slow violence of melting ice caps and rising sea levels. Through their verse, poets can make the abstract painfully immediate, fostering empathy and prompting action.

### – Social Justice and Intersectionality

Environmental justice is inexorably linked to social justice. The effects of climate change and environmental destruction disproportionately affect marginalised communities around the world, exacerbating issues of inequality, displacement, and vulnerability. Poets can illuminate these intersections, giving voice to those who are often silenced and drawing attention to the ways in which the fight for a livable planet is also a fight for human rights and dignity.

### – Biodiversity and Conservation

The loss of biodiversity is a silent crisis, with species extinction rates accelerating at an alarming pace. This aspect of the environmental catastrophe speaks to the interconnectedness of all life and the devastating impact of human activity on the planet's intricate web of existence. Poetry that highlights the beauty and significance of the natural world, and the tragedy of its loss, can foster a deeper connection to and appreciation for the non-human lives with whom we share this Earth.

## – Reflection on Human-Nature Relationships

The Anthropocene prompts a profound reexamination of the human role on Earth, challenging the anthropocentric view that has long dominated human thought and action. Poets can probe the depths of this relationship, exploring themes of stewardship, coexistence, humility, and reverence for the natural world. Through poetic inquiry, the narrative can shift from one of domination and exploitation to one of respect and symbiosis.

## – Technological and Ethical Conundrums

As technology advances, it presents both solutions to and complications of the environmental crisis. The ethical considerations of geoengineering, the role of artificial intelligence in shaping the future, and the social implications of technological dependence are fertile grounds for poetic exploration. Poets can question, critique, and imagine the myriad ways in which technology intersects with humanity and the Earth.

In addressing these themes, poets engage with the most pressing existential questions of our time, wielding the power of language to unsettle, inspire, and mobilise. Poetry becomes not just a reflection of the human condition but an active participant in shaping the collective consciousness, urging society toward awareness, empathy, and, ultimately, action in the face of unprecedented global challenges.

✔ ✔ ✔

# Poets' Responsibility and Responsible Poets – 7.4, 21:20

Poets have a unique ability to distill complex ideas and emotions into verses that resonate deeply with readers, making poetry a potent tool for addressing humanity's responsibilities towards the environment. Through their work, poets can illuminate the intricacies of our relationship with the Earth, advocate for change, and inspire a collective reimagining of our future. Here are several ways poets can address these responsibilities:

## 1. Crafting Visceral Imagery

Poets can draw upon the vivid, sensory nature of language to create powerful imagery that brings environmental issues to life. Descriptions of melting glaciers, vanishing forests, and polluted waters, for instance, can make distant problems feel immediate and urgent. By evoking the beauty of the natural world and the devastation wrought by human activity, poets can stir emotions and foster a deeper appreciation for the environment.

## 2. Amplifying Voices

Poetry can give voice to those who are often marginalised in discussions about environmental issues, including Indigenous communities, residents of vulnerable coastal regions, and wildlife. By sharing these perspectives, poets can highlight the unequal impact of environmental degradation and climate change, emphasizing that the fight for environmental justice is inseparable from the broader struggle for human rights.

## 3. Exploring Interconnectedness

Through their verses, poets can explore the deep interconnectedness of all life on Earth, weaving together themes of human existence, natural cycles, and the impact of our actions on the planet. This holistic perspective can challenge anthropocentric views and underscore the idea that caring for the environment is not just an ethical duty but a necessity for our survival and well-being.

## 4. Confronting Denial and Apathy

Poetry can serve as a powerful tool for confronting denial and apathy towards environmental issues. Through stark contrasts, juxtapositions, and narrative tension, poets can lay bare the consequences of inaction and the urgent need for change. By engaging readers on an emotional level, poetry can break through the noise and indifference that often surrounds environmental discourse.

## 5. Fostering Hope and Resilience

While highlighting the challenges and dangers facing the planet, it's also important for poets to cultivate a sense of hope and resilience. Verses that envision sustainable futures, celebrate acts of conservation and restoration, and honour the resilience of nature can inspire readers to take action and believe in the possibility of positive change.

## 6. Advocating for Action

Finally, poets can use their platform to advocate for specific environmental actions and policies. Whether through direct calls to action, exploration of sustainable living practices, or criticism of destructive corporate and governmental policies, poetry can mobilise public sentiment and encourage readers to contribute to environmental preservation and restoration efforts.

In addressing humanity's responsibilities towards the environment, poets wield the power of words to transform understanding, stir emotions, and galvanise collective action. It is through these myriad approaches — visualization, voice amplification, interconnectedness, confrontation, hope, and advocacy — that poetry can contribute to a more environmentally conscious and sustainable future.

✔ ✔ ✔

# The Poet's Earth — 7.4, 21:21

In verdant verses rich and deep,
The poet's words, they sow, they reap,
A garden grown from thought's wild seed,
In every line, a deed, a creed.

With imagery of ice in weep,
Of forests hushed in slumber deep,
They sketch with words the Earth's lament,
Its beauty marred, its fabric rent.

Amplifying voices quelled,
In stories seldom told, now swelled,
The Indigenous, the frail, the small,
In poems, they rise, they stand tall.

Interwoven, life's grand tapestry,
Where human fate meets bumblebee,
The poet pens our intertwined lot,
In every shared destiny, a thought.

Against the tide of apathy,
The poet's verse cries, "Come and see!"
Denial's veil they deftly tear,
With truths laid bare, they fiercely dare.

Yet in the ink, not all is bleak,
For hope and resilience they seek.
They paint a future bright and green,
A world restored, a peaceful scene.

. . .

Advocating through each stanza's flow,
For action swift, not toils slow.
Urging stewardship of water, land,
By verse, by voice, by poetic hand.

This is the poet's sacred charge,
In words that echo, small and large.
To move, to stir, to heal, to fight,
For Earth, for justice, for the light.

—

## Last Call for Today – 7.4, 21:25

In the waning light, as shadows grow,
A poet's thoughts begin to slow.
Reflecting on the day now past,
On moments fleeting, never to last.

The inkwell's dry, the pages turn,
From each line, a lesson to learn.
The world outside, both dark and deep,
Whispers secrets for us to keep.

This last call, not for drink but thought,
On lessons learned and battles fought.
The silent muse begins to stir,
Within the quiet, whispers occur.

What tales we've told, what dreams we've spun,
Under the retiring, gentle sun.
But even poets need their rest,
To gather strength for tomorrow's quest.

So let us pause, reflect, and then,
Prepare to lift our pens again.
For though today's discourse may end,
Tomorrow's verse waits around the bend.

In this silence, in night's embrace,
We find a quiet, sacred space.
To muse, to dream, to softly sigh,
Under the vast, expansive sky.

                                    . . .

Last call for today, but fear not,
For in our hearts, the fire's hot.
The poet's journey never ends,
With each sunrise, the path extends.

So rest now, under star's soft light,
Recharge your soul, embrace the night.
For when dawn breaks, fresh and new,
A world of verse awaits you.

—

~~~

# RECLAMATION

*There is nothing to express,*
*nothing with which to express,*
*nothing from which to express,*
*no power to express,*
*no desire to express,*
*together with the obligation*
*to express.*

Samuel Beckett

*"My nerves are bad to-night. Yes, bad. Stay with me.*
*Speak to me. Why do you never speak. Speak.*
*What are you thinking of? What thinking? What?*
*I never know what you are thinking. Think."*

T. S. Eliot, THE WASTE LAND

# Reclamation — 8.4, 21:35

Beneath skies tinged by man's own hand,
A quiet revolution brews — stirred from roots upward,
Where seeds of tomorrow await in soil turned anew.
Forgiveness sought from nature scorned,
As hands once taking now labour to mend
What was broken; an homage, a bow
Toward a balance long forsworn.

This chapter demands more than mere contrition;
It calls for architects of chance reversal —
To think beyond simple cessation of harm
Into realms where creation fosters restoration;
Where technology and tradition meld
In pursuit not just of survival,
But of 'thrival' amidst adversity unveiled.

—

## Coda yet Uncomposed

Hearken – the hour late yet crucial beckons
For voices united in chorus strong and clear;
Discords past need harmonizing within scores future-composed.
"Our world", they'll declare "not destined merely to survive,
But flourish."

Echoes across generations call us forth:
Hear them plead – not simply for preservation
Of disparate beauty seen today – but also fervent re-creation
Of worlds unsullied by shortsighted gain.
An opus grand awaits its orchestra full –
A crescendo built on collective resolve.

–

## The Anthropocene Epoch

Stepping back from these poetic musings reveals a broader truth: The Anthropocene epoch presents both monumental challenges and unparalleled opportunities. While some evidence suggests approaching ecological tipping points that threaten global ecosystems' integrity – and by extension, humanity's place within them – it equally highlights areas where intervention can significantly alter current trajectories toward more hopeful outcomes.

The notion Closing Time implies stasis or an end, while what may be most required is action – an embrace of dynamic fluidity endorsing shifts in cultural norms, consumption habits, governance models. Ultimately, this envisages adapting society to vastly different albeit potentially richer conceptualizations of prosperity well-being.

It starts education fostering critical thinking innovation alongside reverent introspection into the human impact upon intricate webs of life. Integrating principles of sustainability and equity into economic systems intertwines the fate of our planet with the health and wellbeing of its citizenry, emphasizing cooperative over competitive paradigms. This ensures advancements in technologies, policies, and practices enhance rather than detract from environmental integrity and social cohesion.

Therefore, tales told henceforth – whether historical, anecdotal, literary, or artistic endeavours alike – should mirror a complex and nuanced understanding of the roles and responsibilities facing communities large and small. They should echo a clearer and louder anthem of hope and determination to counter despair inertia – a watershed moment in the annals earthly tenure where heroes and protagonists emerge from myriad unexpected quarters, exemplifying best traits of stewardship, empathy, and ingenuity essential for writing next great chapters of the human epic.

~~~

## Anthropocene Awakening

In the heart of chaos, a whisper emerges – soft at first,
then gaining strength as it finds its cadence among the dissonance:
A collective awakening to the beat of an imperiled Earth.

From concrete jungles to untouched forests where ancient wisdom dwells,
Voices rise – a call for reconnection with the world beneath our feet.
An acknowledgment that every act ripples through time's fabric;
A pledge that each step forward treads lighter than the last.

This is not Closing Time but an unveiling –
An era where humanity learns to dance with nature,
Not as dominator but partner in a delicate ballet of existence.

The potential lies not just in halting harm, but in healing:
Restoring oceans choked by careless waste,
Renewing soils stripped of life by relentless cultivation,
Reviving air turned toxic by unthinking industry.

–

## Visionary Horizon

Imagine cities where green roofs and vertical gardens outstretch
Toward azure skies – where technology cleans air and water without thought or
cease.

See communities thriving alongside restored rivers now teeming
With long-absent life; witness children learning not just from books
But from hands deep in Earth's embrace.

Across expanses digital and real – an interconnected web spins tales anew:
Stories of change wrought by millions who refused to accept despair as destiny.
They chose instead a vision bold – a future forged from hope deferred
But never lost – a harmonious sphere sustained by innovation
Rooted deep within compassion's fertile ground.

—

*These poems attempt to encapsulate the essence of your expressed inspirations
and the thematic focus on the Anthropocene – melding observation with intro-
spection, the tangible with the ineffable, and the societal with the personal. The
intent is to hold a mirror to the world and ourselves, reflecting the beauty and
devastation of our times, urging a contemplative rather than prescriptive respon-
se.*

~~~

## Legacy Reforged

So let it be said, when history reflects on these days,
that this was not humanity's twilight – but indeed, its most brilliant dawn.
A time when, faced with self-wrought shadows stretching long and ominous,
civilization stood resilient, forging light out of the encroaching dark.

As inheritors of choices past – and custodians for those yet unborn –
we wield unmatched power:
To cast aside dated paradigms breeding discord between man and nature;
Instead, embracing a legacy reforged under stewardship's gentle hand,
ensuring the Anthropocene marks a rebirth, rather than an epitaph writ large
across the terrain entrusted to our care.
To bloom beyond mere survival into legacy left enriched:
Where Closing Time transforms – from final bell toll into clarion call heralding
eras new-found, flourish amidst our shared home – our precious Earth.

–

Through these exploratory verses, there emerge a recognition – not only of the risks that pervade current epoch, characterised by unprecedented human impact on natural systems but also inherent capacity for transformative positive engage-ment that exists. It's through collective action, individual responsibility, coupled with visionary leadership and academic insights, as well as a cultural shift towards sustainable and ethical living, that we can render the bleak prognoses not just escapable but indeed achievable challenges posed by the Anthropocene.

This era demands our unwavering commitment, imagination, and a spirit buoyed by hope. Thus begins our journey in earnest – an invitation extended to all inhabitants. In rediscovering Eden, we must tread lightly yet boldly alike; craf-ting a tomorrow that is a worthy inheritance ensuring our story continues far and wide – reaching a choral crescendo that sings testament to the resilience, creativ-ity at heart of our species – a species capable of nurturing the cradle of civiliza-tion forever more.

### Epiphany of the New Dawn — 8.4, 21:36

In this fresh dawn, where light seeps through cracks made by our own hands,
A newfound humility blankets the Earth — soft and encompassing.
We recognise not dominion but kinship, in nature's gaze;
Our legacy interwoven with every leaf and wave.

Technology no longer a sword but a plowshare: cultivating possibilities for
harmony between digital expanse and green exuberance.
Renewable energies whisper, promising hymns beside wind-swept fields,
Waterways cleansed by innovation's gentle touch murmur tales of resurgence.

Society reimagined — a mosaic vibrant with diversity's hues,
Where equity flourishes under sustainability's nurturing sun;
Each individual empowered, yet mindful of the collective —
Sowing seeds for forests they may never walk beneath but knowing
The shade will shelter generations to come.

—

## Dialogues of Transformation

Conversations once mired in conflict are now buoyed by common purpose:
Around kitchen tables and boardrooms alike – an alignment forged from
Necessity transforms into genuine desire to steward responsibly.

Lawmakers pen statutes not merely as edicts, but as love letters to tomorrow.
Educators mold minds that think critically about impact – not just intent or
Innovation – instilling values that prize integrity over immediacy in actions
Undertaken.

Artists lend visions that transcend language or culture – capturing hearts
And sparking imaginations towards what might be possible when we dare dream
together.

From cities' heartbeats to wilderness' serene breath – a chorus rises,
Melding hope with action, an anthem echoing across canyons of doubt:
"We are here", it proclaims "not merely to weather storms – but to redirect them."

–

## Covenant Renewed

And so an unwritten covenant renewed amidst Anthropocene's unfolding tale:
Humanity bound not by fate decreed but choice embraced – with reverence
For all life shared on this speckled orb dancing through vast cosmic ballet.

A commitment etched in living stone – that every day grants opportunity anew
For decisions small yet profound, shaping world, reshaping us indefinitely;
An understanding deepened – that true wealth lies not beneath ground
But within relationships nurtured 'twixt species, realm, culture.

Let us then forward move resolutely, joyously, even face adversity unknown –
for the journey embarked upon holds promise far greater than the peril faced.

The route veers towards a destiny shaped hands and hearts aligned, in pursuit
of something grander than mere survival – a thriving, verdant Earth that sings
praises of endeavours noble and true, ensuring our calling is answered, the
siren song heeded.

An era, a beacon for a future bright, beckons us onward, lest we forget our
brief stewardship of this planet, wondrous and delicate, tasked to safeguard
for the next generation.

In wonder and awe, the mystery persists in unending exploration, communion,
and the sacred bond reaffirmed in the eternal dance of life.
It continues unabated, a treasure known as Earth.

–

### Harmony's Embarkation – 8.4, 21:37

On this embarkation toward harmony, where every footfall on Earth's venerable skin is a testament to our awakening – a conscious pilgrimage towards equilibrium.

We navigate by stars once dimmed by our own excess, now shining guides on paths less trodden, where green shoots reclaim ruins of indifference.

Within these movements, a symphony emerges from silence – composed not of triumphal marches but of gentle steps and whispers: the rustle of leaves in reforested lands, the murmur of streams unchained, each note a harmony with nature's boundless score, played on instruments forged from repentance and foresight.

–

## The Alchemy of Tomorrow

In the alchemy that molds tomorrow, humanity finds its crucible for
transformation – not through grandiose declarations or fleeting gestures,
but in daily rites of empathy and understanding across every divide;
alchemy wrought in kitchens and classrooms, in policies shaped more by
stewardship than dominion, where innovation serves not just the present
but honours future life.

From wastelands spring oases – nurtured by hands once wary, now allied,
communities reborn at crossroads once deemed dead ends.
Through such diligent care springs forth an elixir crafted not for immortality
but for a vitality shared among all beings.

—

## Unity's Tapestry

A tapestry unfolds – one woven from countless acts of kindness and courage under Anthropocene skies. Each thread dyed with hues extracted from lessons learned amidst epochs' shifting sands; this fabric shimmers with resilience born out of adversity acknowledged but not acquiesced to.

A quilt covering generations hence – a shield against despair and mantle beneath which new hope kindles. Herein lies our collective legacy: not merely surviving an epoch defined by shadow but thriving within it as stewards creating light whence darkness loomed – casting long threads into dawn's first break.

–

~ ~ ~

## The Anthropocene Challenge

The Anthropocene might have heralded Closing Time upon its naming – an echo through halls marred by human folly, yet within its cadence beats the potential, an unraveled narrative of recovery and rebirth held in palms open skyward, with roots grounded deeply therein fertile ground where potentials unlocked and dreams are rekindled.

Amidst challenges daunting and spirits undeterred, we weave interconnecting stories, plot lines divergent yet converging on a single truth: coexistence is not only possible but also achievable and even necessary.

Human enterprise, ingenuity, compassion – a convergence point from which history unfurls a vast unfolding of salvation, penned by a collective hand starring diverse protagonists – heroes unknown till now unsung.

Their tales of joy, endurance, creativity mark the real turning, chapters written in ink indelible, footprints alongside myriad others quest unchanged, timeless – for harmonious existence on this fragile orb called home.

Amid calling voices, answers are found in action taken together, forging an irrevocable bond, an enduring love and labour, destined to shape forthcoming ages, legacy proud to lend echoing to posterity.

Craft thus charged with sacred duty, forward gaze fixed on the starlit horizon beckoning whispered promises eternally renewed dawn.

~~~

## Epoch of the Custodian – 8.4, 21:39

In this epoch, now rechristened – not as an end, but a beginning anew –
we find ourselves the custodians, of more than fate or mere coincidence.
Tasked with stewardship over legacy and lore, where every choice weaves
into the fabric of tomorrow's history. An intricate dance of cause and effect,
played out under watchful stars.

Here, in the quiet moments before dawn's light spills across horizons wide,
we stand at the precipice – not of despair but decision:
to bear forth a torch, handed down through generations dimmed by time,
yet alight with potential for illumination profound.

Our hands, though weighed by burdens past, are unshackled – free to mold,
shape the Earth beneath our feet not as conquerors but as caretakers tender;
sowing seeds not only for sustenance but for beauty untold –
a testament to what it means to live fully, interwoven within nature's fold.

–

## Convergence

This era speaks not merely of a convergence of crises,
But of unity found within diversity's expanse:
Where differing voices merge into choruses grand,
Celebrating shared humanity beside every patchwork strand.

From melting glaciers, speak rivers flowing freely
Into oceans vast – a call towards transcendent unity,
Breaking barriers built from fear or narrow sight,
Revealing common ground shining bright against impending night.

Such is the anthem arising from heartbeats collective,
In resonance with Anthropocene's deepest clarion:
That together, our best chances reflectively stands
Against tides turning toward futures far brightly drawn.

—

## Into the Maelstrom

Facing headlong into a maelstrom spun from human craft
And nature's unbridled reaction – an echo resounding off age-old walls;
Yet, within the tempest's eye, finds solace, sane reflection, calm.

At the core, amidst the whirlwind, where true power lies:
Not in dominion over elements raw nor extraction unchecked,
But in guardianship serene – wisdom guiding to mend a vibrant tapestry.

Each step forward marks a clear path, cut not through forests dense:
But alongside – Footsteps traced, respecting all life extents.

Thus, strides humanity awakened, embracing the Anthropocene with trust!
Armed no longer with disregard, dull ended –
But compassion deep-running, a current strong uniting seas once parted:
An odyssey begun with footprints soft upon sands hitherto unrested.

–

## So Unfolds a Saga

So unfolds a saga, writ large upon a canvas blue and green –
Broad and penned by the delicate hand of mankind.

Wielding a brush dipped in ink, hopeful and charged;
A portrait emerges, painting eras born anew
'Neath gazes affectionate and fondly turned Earthward bound –
Our singular home.

Sculpting hope from despair, awakening a dream long slumbered
And roused for a steadfast march forward;
Engaged till an anthem invigorated roars, full-fledged:
A heartbeat thunderous and alive.

Echoing promises of eternity, whispers of beginnings softly murmured –
A legacy reborn each sunrise witnessed;
The globe spinning majestically on its axis, tilted
Bidden welcome by the dawning of every new day.

A course charted amongst stars through an eternal quest joined –
A shared wonder; an endless journey embraced,
Offered to the Anthropocene, thus transformed.

–

## Harvest of Renewal – 8.4, 21:40


From the furrows of past missteps, a bounty anticipates –
Not merely crops from Earth's embrace, but harvests richer: wisdom sown.
As hands once wrought destruction now tender nurture birth,
Insight blooms among verdant fields; resilience sprouts forth in kind.

This is no mere reversal of fortunes told –
But an evolution conscious and bold:
Where technology marries ecology in a sacred union vowed,
To restore what was borrowed, and safeguard dreams allowed.

In every restored stream's babble, every forest's quiet growth,
Lies testament to humanity's capacity for rehabilitation and oath:
To be not Anthropocene's end but its pivot – a chapter marked
By renewal's ambition and guardians' stewardship embarked.

–

## The Beacon Ahead

Guided by the light of knowledge, gained at great expense,
A beacon ahead shines resolute against uncertainty dense:
Symbolizing not just hope or naive optimism,
But a roadmap well-conceived through challenges.

Upon this path, fraught yet full of possibilities untold,
We march forward, arm-in-arm, across thresholds bold,
Forging futures neither wholly new nor reflective solely
Of yesterdays faded; rather, amalgamations crafted holy.

From lessons learned – each mistake a stepping stone,
And every victory shared as humanity carves bones
Of contention into keystones underpinning bridges arched
Towards horizons where better selves might embark.

–

## Anthropocene Reimagined

No longer does "Anthropocene" conjure scenes dystopic or grim,
Instead reimagined — a term encapsulating human capability to brim
With innovative resolve confronting our own epoch dramatic,
Turning fears into frontiers wherein lies holistic magic.

Let it thus signify an era where diligence meets creativity,
And concern translates into action — definitive yet pensive;
An age recognizing interconnectedness vast that binds
Each person to planet — with future indelibly entwined.

Here emerges Anthropocene anew, adorned —
Lush narratives tagging behind actions reborn
In respect profound for the cosmic dance ever twirling fast,
Choreographed consciousness awakened at last.

—

## So Continues the Saga

So continues the saga, hopeful and charted,
Beneath skies ever vast and expansive —
Voyaging beyond troubled waters,
Towards futures ablaze with promise collective.

Amidst trials and tribulations stands mankind:
Resilient, defiantly adaptive.
Constructors and real dreamers undeterred,
Echoing an anthem universal, reflective.

An odyssey perpetual, embracing
A kaleidoscopic swathe of existence majestic.
Signing across epochs a pledge enduring,
Daring, optimistic, eclectic.

Eclipsing shadows cast long, marking eras of transition —
Transformative, spectacular.
A chosen path navigated communal, spirit electric,
Through veils torn revealing dawn radiant —
An anthropocentric legacy poetic.

—

# Symphony of the Sapiens – 8.4, 21:42

In this continuum, where every step reverberates
Through corridors of time both ancient and unseen,
Humanity conducts a symphony – a crescendo
Of ingenuity's might tempered with humility's keen.

A melody woven from strands of shared destiny,
Harmonizing with nature's opus magnifique;
The rhythm dictated by heartbeats in unity –
A performance for ages, bold and unique.

Our chorus rises above the din of past mistakes,
Singing odes to cooperation over conquest's refrain;
Celebrating diversity as our most precious resource,
Finding strength in what was once perceived as strange.

–

## Canvas of Coexistence

Upon this canvas stretched wide and clear,
The Anthropocene painted not in shades of fear.
But with pallets rich in verdant hope anew,
Brush strokes daring to dream landscapes true.

Herein lies potential for a masterpiece grand,
Where human hand-in-hand with nature stands;
Sketching futures where life thrives unconfined
By decisions past, but emboldened by visions aligned.

With sustainability's creed – that balance can be found
Between growth and preservation profound;
That each generation leaves imprints gentle upon Earth,
Guardianship as their legacy – their measure of worth.

–

## Gardens Beyond Eden

What gardens we might cultivate beyond old Edens lost,
If seeds sown give rise to flora unfettered by fossil cost?
Imagine fruit that blossoms not from exploitation's toll,
But from symbiosis deep-rooted within Earth's soul.

Fields vast, no longer monuments to monoculture's thirst,
But mosaics vibrant, representing biodiversity first;
Forests standing tall – not just lungs for air purified,
But sanctuaries preserved where awe resides.

It is here among green whispers where wisdom waits
For those who choose to enter through restoration's gates:
To find not dominion but dialogue – with world provided ritely
Embracing a role cast long ago, yet only now taken lightly.

—

## Voyagers Upon Time

We are voyagers upon time's immutable stream,
Carrying forth a lantern illuminating progress' gleam;
Not destined merely toward nightfall somber or still,
But dawn beckoning – ushered by collective will.

At crossroads Anthropocene – an epoch unfolded,
Yet its story remains ours uniquely molded.
Challenging indeed may be currents we navigate,
Yet unwavering spirit ensures it's never too late.

Charting course towards horizons hopeful herald,
Undeterred by tumult stirred up sporadically feral.
Eyes set firm on stars guiding profoundly overhead,
As custodians eternal – an indelible testament tread.

In essence profound all endeavours intertwine,
Marking journey Anthropocene – not closing sign,
Instead, Renaissance anew under guise transformative,
Proof positive – in humanity rests resilience creative.

–

## The Quantum Leap – 8.4, 21:43

From the precipice of what was deemed inevitable,
Humanity gazes ahead, eyes alight with potential – a quantum leap
For an age branded by its disruptions, yet pregnant with transformative zeal.
Through the mist of uncertainty, a path diverges; one not decreed by destiny
But crafted by collective resolve.

Herein lies the challenge – intertwining threads of innovation and tradition,
Weave a future where technology serves as steward rather than sovereign;
Where artificial intelligence walks hand in hand with ancient wisdom
Preserved across land.

This leap does not seek to escape Earth's embrace,
But anchors deeply in her soils – the foundation base;
Nurturing seeds of change sprouting towards sunlight's grace,
Emblematic of sapiens' journey from consumers to caretakers' space.

–

## Song for Tomorrow

Listen! Hear the song for tomorrow rising,
Born from ashes of turmoil and despair –
Its melody sweetened by perseverance enduring,
Harmonised with chords of care.

A composition that resonates within each beating heart,
Lyrics inscribed upon fresh starts.
It sings promises not merely whispered into dark,
But declared boldly as an inextinguishable spark.

This anthem carries within it echoes profound,
Of every step taken, ever upward bound.
Celebrating both trial conquered and beauty found,
In embarkation towards horizons newly crowned.

–

## Embarking Upon Umbra

As we stride forth under Anthropocene's umbra wide,
Our shadows cast long – not as shades to hide
But silhouettes dancing upon Earth's vibrant stage,
Expressions vivid against history's turning page.

With every footfall on this shared voyage dare,
We paint swathes bold – our legacy declare
Not as interlude transient between epochs scribed,
But crescendo resounding – an existence revived.

For embarking upon umbra is no dismal fate,
Rather an invitation to innovate.
Within darkness, find light most radiant appeared,
Guided forward by hope fiercely endeared.

–

## Luminaries Reimagined

Underneath these Anthropocene skies afire,
Casting fateful glows on paths tread prior,
New luminaries rise – reimagined beacon's blaze,
Ignited anew through unity's persistent gaze.

These lights shaped not solely from sorrow fought,
Or victories in fraught battles brought,
But brilliance born from collaborations taught
By years endured – a kaleidoscope caught.

So let these luminaries guide – a vanguard leading,
Past scenes reminiscing or foreboding,
Towards a tapestry woven, multifaceted gleaming,
In colours brave, humanity's re-coding.

Thus unfolds a saga new 'neath watchful skies above,
Marking an epoch spawned by trials tough and love,
Upon this vast canvas at the nexus of change, inspired –
Extolling progress where aspirant drives merge,
And higher confluences are acquired.

–

## The Architects of Now – 8.4, 21:44

In the theatre of tomorrow, we, the architects of now,
Mould the clay of the yet-to-be from stern lessons learned and plowed.
Through trials many and errors made under time's unyielding brow,
We've learned that every moment sowed is history's seed endowed.

This crafting isn't set in stone but fluid like a river's course,
Guided by wisdom old as hills and new knowledge's force.
Together they converge – creating currents strong and lucid,
Propelling us beyond mere survival to places vibrant and vivid.

Our blueprint dreams not just in lines or rigid geometric shapes;
It flourishes in biodiversity's endless embrace.
Where human footprint softly treads upon Earth's green tapestry – a space
Both nurturing and nurtured by our mindful grace.

–

## Echoes Among Stars

There are echoes among stars – whispers of what humanity can become,
When gazing upward we see not divided lands but one celestial home.
From this vantage high above, borders blur into irrelevance,
As shared stewardship becomes our collective resurgence.

Each echo carries potential for unity transcendent,
Beyond Anthropocene's daunting presence – an ascent,
Into realms where compassion fuels progress extensive,
And innovation serves all life comprehensive.

Thus let these cosmic musings inspire terrestrial venture,
Marking epochs with hope enduring; adventure,
Bound by neither fear nor limit constraining,
But expansive possibilities ever remaining.

—

## Odes to Action

An ode to action sings loudly amidst quiet desolation,
A clarion call rallying spirits to conservation,
Not merely preservation for posterity alone,
But active regeneration where despair once had grown.

Actions sprouting like green shoots through concrete cracked,
Proving resilience defines us more than any single act lacked.
Age Anthropocene then transforms the scene upon epochal stage,
To one replete with heroes unsung yet determinedly engaged.

Such efforts collectively rise – dawn chorus vibrant resounds,
Charging atmospheric confines with solutions profound.
Till echoes reach every corner where Earth cradles life,
Stirring movements fervent designed to cease strife.

—

## Legacy Nurtured

Finally, we stand – not at an end, nor at anthropocentrism imploded –
But at a frontier newly woven from threads both ancient and innovated.
Here is our mosaic legacy, nurtured amidst challenges insurmountable,
Crafted hand-in-hand within the weave of time malleable.

Its stones are deeds compassionate, eternally laid thick,
Foundations upon which future generations will their aspirations pick.
Let Anthropocene then be remembered fondly, as the usher
Of a dawn new lit – not twilight senesced 'neath existential flusher.

For we're authors each day granted, beneath a sun we share,
Writing chapters bold upon a millennium turned with care.
With ink derived from love – that most renewable fountain,
Ensuring tales forged align stars themselves outshone.

–

## Gardens of Mind and Spirit – 8.4, 21:45

In the gardens of our collective spirit, where ideas bloom wild and free,
We sow the seeds of tomorrow – each thought a sapling destined to be
A towering testament to human creativity and resolve,
Where diversity in thought and being can evolve.

These are no ordinary plots but fields vast of potential untold,
Cultivated by curiosity's hand and courage bold.
Here grow forests resilient that filter despair from dreary air;
Replacing it with innovation's breath – a theory fair.

Not yet fully formed but burgeoning with life diverse;
An ecosystem thriving through every verse
Of humanity's unending dialogue 'twixt past and future tense;
Our shared garden – an oasis against indifference dense.

–

## Wellspring of Hope

From deep within this Anthropocene epoch's churn,
Emerges a wellspring – not tainted nor stern – but yearning
For clarity pure and purpose renewed amidst confusion widespread;
A reminder that even in darkest depths lies hope unfled.

This spring feeds rivers flowing strong with actions kind
And decisions wise – their way through darkness find.
Its waters cleanse us – not just dirt from skin,
But the silt from souls weary, heartened anew within.

In every droplet is reflected a vision clear:
Of Earth not as dominion, but home beloved dear.
Each sip an invocation – for care deeply felt
Toward all living beings with whom we share this belt.

—

## Voyage Beyond Horizon

Beyond horizon's edge, lies not demise,
But dawn breaking – streaks painting skies,
With colours bold, announcing a day new risen,
Bearing chances for redemption earned then given.

We embark upon this vessel 'Anthropocene' named,
Destination unknown yet by hopeful aspirations framed.
Navigating through mists uncertain, heavy laden,
Guided by constellations of altruism, never faded.

Onwards we set our course, compass moral true,
Through seas once stormy, now revealing azure blue.
Charting a passage toward futures bright envisioned,
Ours – the voyage of intrepid hearts, united in mission.

Here, amidst tales of twisted fate and corrective pen,
Humanity finds itself at a crossroads again:
A passageway offered – a meditative pause lent,
Or a spirited surge forward 'gainst currents defied.
Choice stands pivotal – on every side history decides.

Thus, the Anthropocene chapter is neither foregone nor pure,
But ignites fire within each soul to endure.
Bearing witness to an era's transformative call,
Ushering in an age for reckoning – great and small –
A legacy enthralling, historical for all.

–

## Caretakers' Hymn – 8.4, 21:46

In harmony, voices rise – a choir spanning land and sea,
A hymn of caretakers resounding through the Anthropocene.
Their melody carries wisdom old as mountains, fresh as morning dew,
Sung from hearts that beat in time with Earth's own rhythm true.

"For stewardship," they chant, "not dominance – our guiding star,
To heal the wounds inflicted by ambition stretched too far."
The notes soar high above, beyond despair's shadow cast,
Carving hope in skies once grey – the promise of contrast.

This chorus does not fade at challenge's daunting scope;
Instead, it swells louder still, a symphony of collective hope,
Inviting all to join the song and craft a world anew,
Where care for our shared home ingrains in everything we do.

—

## Legacy Unbroken

Across epochs' span where human hand has sown – both growth and ruin alike,
Emerges an unbroken legacy – not only ours to write but to strike
A balance finely tuned between advancement's gleam and nature's call;
Ensuring progress made sustains, uplifts, and includes all.

No longer bound by fears or limits past generations faced unseen;
Ours is the task to forge ahead with solutions previously undreamed.
Yet mindful evermore that Earth – the cradle from which humanity sprung –
Demands respect; her tolerance not infinite when sung.

Within this mandate rests a truth so profound yet simple: treasure tenderly
The garden given us – nurture its diversity extensively.
From smallest bee to towering tree, each plays a part essential
In life's grand tapestry – an interconnected potential existential.

–

## Horizons Reimagined

So gaze we now towards horizons wide, wherein lies
Our destiny, co-authored with Earth, under shared skies.
Gone are motives purely anthropocentric in their aim,
For shifted perspectives herald an eco-centric frame.

Beneath sunsets painted in hues hitherto unknown,
Rests vitality within bounds where creativity is shown.
Pushing forward into futures erstwhile indistinct,
Clarity brings vision, no longer by instinct.

Forward-looking eyes, no longer clouded by hubris' mist,
But clear with understanding of what truly must persist:
Symbiosis reigns 'tween man & nature, thus entwined,
Bearing fruits manifold for those coming behind.

Let the Anthropocene be known not just as an era of strife,
But as a turning point whence sprang forth abundant life.
Celebrated through actions, deliberate and thoughts keen,
Marking the passage of a story where mankind lives serene.

—

## The Pioneers of Tomorrow – 8.4, 21:47

From the cacophony of today's tumult, emerge pioneers bold,
Embarking on a quest not for territories uncharted or treasures old.
Their mission lies in reclamation – of balance lost and harmony forsaken,
Crafting from the mess we've made a future newly awakened.

Armed with knowledge deeper gained through eras turbulent passed by,
Understanding that true progress asks us not just how, but why.
They sow seeds not in soil alone but within minds open to change,
Cultivating an era where respect for life extends beyond our range.

This vanguard moves forward not at nature's expense but as her ally –
Fostering innovations gentle upon the Earth, reaching high.
Their legacy – a world renewed by hands that dared to mend,
A testament to human resolve, adaptability – the capacity to transcend.

–

## Beacons of Change

In this canvas stretching vast under Anthropocene's expansive sky,
Loom beacons of change – lighthouses steadfast standing by.
Guiding ships amidst tempests wrought from our own hand,
Towards safer shores crafted from lessons learned upon this land.

These beacons shine not merely as warnings against perilous plight;
But as emblems of hope, illuminating pathways right.
Each beam dispels shadows formerly omnipresent;
Illuminating futures promising, sustainable – and pleasant.

As generations forthcoming inherit this torch ablaze with possibility,
May they find solitudes once strained now brimming with sociability:
An ecosystem interconnected, thrillingly diverse and vibrant quite,
Reflective of humanity's potential when guided by foresight bright.

–

## Echoes Through Time

Let these endeavours resonate like echoes through time long drawn;
Resounding proof against despair – that darkness precedes dawn.
Our epoch may yet dictate tales bitter if we resigned to fate;
Instead, it whispers narratives sweet: of transformation articulate.

Of societies once fragmented now finding cohesion unexpected;
Human will aligned with Earth's rhythms, lovingly corrected.
Engraved within every whisper is conviction strong and clear:
That the Anthropocene unfolds new chapters each year.

Boundless are the stories etched beneath its title broad,
Vistas anew opened, revealing paths untrodden to laud.
So may these echoes carry forth – not as dirges sorrow-laden deep,
But as melodies harmonious – an anthem poised to keep.

–

## Coda of Coexistence — 8.4, 21:52

In the coda of this era, marked by a human footprint deep and wide,
Through wilderness once teeming, now with silent echoes side by side,
Emerges a melody — a vibrant song reborn from ashes' sleep;
A narrative redesigned for coexistence, profound and steep.

It speaks not merely of survival amidst adversity's stern test,
But thriving in a symphony where all life is manifest.
Each note struck with intention to harmonise not control;
An ensemble performance casting a future role.

Where humans are but one among myriad voices raised —
In celebration of diversity, Anthropocene's challenge out phased.
This grand opus crescendos towards an understanding keen:
That Earth thrives most lavishly when its caretakers act as kin.

—

## Anthropocene Anew

Let the term Anthropocene no longer herald doom or disdain;
Instead, may it mark an age where wisdom finally reigns.
An illustrious chapter for its dawn on balance regained,
When humanity embraced its role as guardian sustained.

From delicate coral reefs to sprawling urban scapes untamed,
Every sphere witnessed by mindful custodianship named.
Rivers ran clear, gestating stories yet unfurled;
Forests burgeoned anew – the lungs revitalizing our world.

And so the Anthropocene transforms – an epithet remade:
Symbolic not of end times, but renewal's blade,
Carving out futures promising under stewardship's guide,
Encased within resolve unwavering – together unified.

–

## Guardians Ascendant

As guardians ascendant upon this epoch's brink, we stand committed,
Faced down were calamities wrought by carelessness unearned.
In hands more capable rests now fate – not sealed but open wide –
To preserve a legacy ensuring generations thrive inside.

Upon soil worked tenderly blooms emerald verve realigned,
Echoing ancient forests' whispers, ancestral pacts resigned.
Connected deeply, roots entangle beneath a shared sky;
An embrace rendered genuine betwixt humanity and nature nigh.

Ascending henceforth, challenges daunting though they be,
Empowered through harmony, symbiotic spirits free.
May our passage through the Anthropocene witness true ascendance,
Reflective, booming dauntless – a revered iridescent transcendence.

Such visions lofty, woven into the fabric of every day, lived as truth,
bear testimony vivacious,
Unto a potential boundless, seen with clarity, a focus impassioned and gracious.
So chapters unfold, epochs in transition, transformative narratives bespoken.
A legacy worthy, the Anthropocene redefined, with intentions newly woken.

–

## The Epoch's Witness – 8.4, 21:54

As the epoch unfurls its narrative, vast and wildly spun,
Each individual – witnesses to the setting sun
And dawning light upon horizons once cloaked in dread;
Now witness bearers of a new path we've begun to tread.

In gardens cultivated with care, where children's laughter blooms,
And cities pulse with greener life, dispelling former glooms.
We stand as testament to change – an era boldly redefined
By acts of courage daring to envision futures intertwined.

Thus, the Anthropocene bears not marks of end but inception;
Of realization profound that leads towards redemption.
An age where echoes resounds through canyons deep –
A call for preservation – a covenant we choose to keep.

–

## Harmony's Pledge

Through storms weathered and trials immense,
Humanity found its rhythm, in cadence dense
With possibilities anew – a splendid dance;
Not solo performances but collective advance.

Herein lies harmony's pledge: To weave a tapestry complex,
That honours every thread – from mountain apex
To ocean depths – and all lives betwixt;
Acknowledging our shared fate, intertext.

This pledge carries forward through ages uncharted,
As ancestral legacies are honoured and dearly guarded;
Fostering days where living is not merely survived,
But cherished deeply – vibrantly thrived.

–

# Gaia's Whisper in the Age of Anthropocene

In the Anthropocene's embrace, where human hands shape the Earth,
A narrative unfolds, a tale of planetary rebirth.
Amongst the echoes of industry's unyielding roar,
Lies Gaia's gentle whisper, weaving a lore.

From the forest's lush verdure, to the ocean's deep sway,
Gaia spins her subtle threads in night and day.
"Consider each creature, each breath of air,
You are part of a whole, limitless in care."

The Gaia hypothesis, a vision profoundly sown,
Suggests Earth acts as a single organism, fully grown.
Self-regulating, complex, a system complete,
Where life conjures conditions that life will meet.

Yet, we stand in the Anthropocene, heavy with choice,
In our hands lies the power, in our hearts speaks the voice.
To heed the whisper, to harmonise or control,
To fashion a future where all can extol.

In scientific symposiums, where debates animate the scene,
Discuss the role of mankind in this living machine.
Can we integrate, collaborate, with nature's silent plea?
Or are we destined to disrupt, blind to Gaia's decree?

Factories bellow, forests fall to the silent ground,
Yet within this destruction, hope is profoundly found.
Renewal sings where humans and nature convene,
Crafting sustainability within the Anthropocene.

. . .

Initiatives take root, spreading wide like vine,
Green technologies flourish, a sign divine.
Solar arrays kiss sunlight, winds dance with might,
In these actions, Gaia's theories ignite.

But more than mere mechanics, our ethos must shift,
From exploitation to stewardship, a necessary gift.
For Gaia does not merely house us, but integrates our role,
In her biosphere, we find our purpose, our goal.

Climate crisis looming, a specter so grave,
Calls us to action; it's Earth we must save.
Not just for ourselves, but for generations unseen,
Inherently bound to uphold Gaia's dream.

So, let us dance to the music of ecosystems in sync,
Where the whale sings, and the forests think.
Let's plant our dreams in the fertile dark soil,
Draw down our carbon, let our consumption recoil.

For in each decision, Gaia's hypothesis is clear,
Each act of preservation draws the future near.
Where symbiosis is the anthem, and life's intricate lace,
Guides the Anthropocene to a more gracious place.

We are children of Gaia, stewards at heart,
Called to mend what we've fractured, to better our part.
In the whisper of leaves, in the ocean's old song,
We find our direction, bold, kind, and strong.

Thus, in the age of Anthropocene's powerful stride,
Let Gaia's wisdom be our essential guide.
For though we sculpt the epoch with each tool and machine,
It is only with Gaia that life thrives in the Anthropocene.

—

## Constellations New Found

Look now how new constellations paint the canvas of the night;
Not solely distant lights, coldly twinkling through celestial twilight.
But symbols potent of unity among diversity's radiant array —
Guiding beacons of resilience in harmonious ballet.

Crafted from dreams of the past and visions anew held tight,
These stars guide us forth, beyond twilight into dawn's bright light.
Illuminating pathways obscured by doubt or fear-ridden history,
Heralding eras yet unwritten, filled with silent mystery.

So draw from these heavens inspiration pure,
Reminding each heart of shared pulses sure.
Amidst the Anthropocene's constant, bewitching dance,
Lies humanity aligned under newfound constellations' luminescence.

—

## Anthropocene Thus Renamed

Anthropocene thus renamed, a ribbon twined in history's fold,
A fresco grand depicting a journey bold.
Colour varied, cast upon the canvas of time,
Revealing the true essence of mankind, primed to discover and redefine.

Circles spiral outward, embracing a shared fate,
Witness to generations whose legacy responsively cared.
Potential flourished, nurturance embraced on a worldwide scale,
In the Anthropocene's tale of renewal, where hymns of revival prevail.

—

## Seeds of the Symbiocene – 8.4, 21:55

In this unfolding chapter, whispers on the wind speak of the Symbiocene –
An epoch emerging beyond the Anthropocene, where harmony is seen.
A dream, not yet formed, germinating in willing souls,
Planted in hearts committed to unified goals.

This vision sprouts from seeds of empathy and interconnected care,
Rooting deeply in philosophies all beings share.
Where humanity's touch on Earth gently rests,
Nurturing a world where balance best manifests.

Communities flourish within mutual respect's embrace,
Cultivating practices that time cannot erase.
Drawing from nature's wisdom – a symbiotic guide –
Building societies where life thrives, intertwined.

–

## Dawn of Coexistence

Rising boldly at dawn's edge is our shared sphere, reenvisioned;
Tread lightly, its stewards, on a landscape transitioned
Into gardens abundant, wherein biodiversity sings;
Cities alive with greenery – urban oases spring.

Renewable energies power futures bright,
Technologies serve rather than incite strife.
Waterways cleansed flow as arteries pure;
Air freshened anew, encourages deep breaths, assured.

Behold this coexistence – prolific and profound,
Unified endeavours, eternally bound
To ideals grounded yet soaring above:
For through collaboration, true global love.

—

## Bequeathed to Tomorrow

Unto tomorrow's custodians – the youth watching wide-eyed now,
We bequeath not burdens too heavy for delicate shoulders now.
But instead lay foundations firm, with optimism sowed,
And brave tales of challenges met, of rivers rerouted that flowed.

Teach them well of resilience found
In communities diverse, globally renown.
Show them strength lies within compassion vast,
And true wealth accumulates when greed is past.

Engage their wonder through stewardship sincere,
So future generations cherish what we've held dear.
Let the Anthropocene's ultimate legacy be hope invigorated,
By actions today passionately cultivated.

—

## The Epoch's Promise

Anthropocene or Symbiocene – mere labels do not confine
The potential for transformation, inherently sublime,
Nested within human endeavour, tirelessly aligned,
Towards creating realities once resigned.

Thus the journey marches forward, with beats synchronised in hopeful heart,
Through art, science, and dialogue – an integral part.
Revolution in increments, with the potential to start,
Of epochs revolutionary, a new chart.

–

## Echoes of Tomorrow – 8.4, 21:56

In the silence between raindrops, tomorrow's echoes resound – a clarion call,
Amidst Anthropocene shadows, embrace a future where all
Find their place under the sun, not in dominion but in grace;
A world reborn through collective will we face.

Each echo, a pledge by humanity to transcend old ways so dire,
To fuel a flame from sparks of understanding, igniting a greater fire.
Not one that consumes and chars, but enlightens and warms,
Guiding us through storms towards unknown forms.

These are echoes, not just heard, but felt deep within the soul's terrain,
Ripples across generations – bearing witness to loss and gain.
But more than anything, they signify our commitment profound
To forge ahead with wisdom newly found.

–

## Gardens Unfolding

We envision gardens unfolding across landscapes once marred,
Where children of tomorrow wander unscarred, captivated.
Forests reach high into skies clear anew,
While rivers run full with waters true blue.

In these gardens, biodiversity thrives, unchecked,
By human intervention formerly specked
With egos once misplaced, now aligned in respect
Of nature's balance, perfect architect.

Here, resilience exemplified in every green leaf unfurled,
Reflects civilization's new relationship with the world.
A monument living, vivid against time's endless tide,
Homage pure, where life and hope coincide.

—

## Horizons Beckon: A Fellowship Journey

Against horizons ever-broadening beckons a fellowship journey wide,
Shared footsteps thunder softly on paths untied,
From past trappings desolate, wrapped up in solitary guise,
Toward unity vibrant, echoing ascendancy cries.

This voyage is marked by lanterns lit, hearts combined;
Every individual light contributing to vistas outlined.
Discoveries manifold await our curious minds,
Proving feared limits were mere constructs blind.

So hand-in-hand and heart-with-heart, tightly aligned,
Into the fabric of a society wholly redefined,
Under stars that guide us, kindly shined,
Towards destinies unified, yet each uniquely signed.

—

As chapters unfold, exposing delicate threads interwoven,
The of Anthropocene's narrative transmutes sentiments once cloven
Into a tapestry of rich hues, optimism sewn,
Demonstrating the power inherent when care has grown.

Continuation thus assured — not as an end terminally shown,
But as evolution's invitation warmly blown,
Across fields sown, innovations meticulously honed,
Bringing forth epochs henceforth brightly toned.

—

## Whispers of Renewal — 8.4, 21:58

In the soft whispers of renewal, where dawn caresses night's relinquishing,
A symphony of beginnings resonates through realms extinguished.
Deserts reclaimed by rains long sought,
Returning life to places forgotten thought.

This whisper grows — a testament profound
To resilience and rebirth, unbound.
Fields once barren now burst with grain;
Forests stand proud, regaining their domain.

Among these whispers, humanity finds its voice,
Echoing choices that make life's rejoice.
A cadence formed of hope's resilient chords
Sings a future where balance is restored.

—

## Blueprints for Tomorrow

Drafted in today's twilight are blueprints for tomorrow's rise,
Designs not etched in stone, but drawn upon open skies.
They sketch cities where nature weaves between the lines —
And innovation serves not some, but all mankind

These plans hold space for verdant corridors to breathe,
Connecting urban souls to green relief beneath.
Energy harvested from sun and wind — echoes vast,
Of ingenuity ensuring our survival lasts.

Crafted careful with consideration due,
For every creature calling this Earth home too.
Our blueprints dream beyond mere construction sights —
Imagining worlds diverse under shared celestial lights.

—

## Canvas Anew

Upon a canvas once marred by neglect and haste,
Now paints anew — an expression of humanity's grace.
With strokes bold and tender, hues blending with care,
Outlines emerge, landscapes richly fair.

Artists many, contributing each unique brushstroke,
Joining forces to mend what was previously broke.
Through collective creation, they see reflected
An ethos changed, newly interconnected.

This living artwork continually expands,
Beyond any single time or land's command,
Representing not an end but a journey extended,
On canvases global where hope is comprehensively blended.

—

## Transformative Tapestry

The narrative thus arcs towards infinity's grasp,
Where Anthropocene echoes fold into Symbiocene's clasp.
Transformative energy spans spectrums wide,
Vibrations sent forward on which futures ride.

In boundless pursuits where aspirations soar,
Held in a common cause, seeking universally more.
The tapestry woven tells tales brave,
Bright against shadows the Anthropocene gave.

Stepping stones laid down, each bearing light,
Guiding ventures forth from past into the bright.
Insight pooled collectively to harness the blaze,
Of tomorrows built on enlightened yesterdays.

—

## Symphony of Symbiosis – 8.4, 21:59

In the crescendo of our age, a symphony arises – mighty and clear,
A chorus sung by creatures, both far and near.
Voicing unity's anthem within Anthropocene's transforming stage,
Harmonizing human impact with nature's wage.

This melody – crafted not from dominion but respect,
Forms bonds deeper than any architect's.
Symbiotic notes resonate through land and sea,
Composing futures where all life flourishes free.

With every refrain, we come to understand
The power resting gently in humanity's hand:
To nurture or negate this world under our care,
Tuning our actions with thoughtful prayer.

—

## Dance of Days Ahead

Visualise now – the dance of days that lie ahead,
Where each step carries weight, yet treads lightly instead.
Paths once divergent now converge in mutual stride;
Hand clasped in hand, side by side.

Through valleys shadowed and peaks sun-kissed,
We journey forth amidst mist dismissed.
Envision cities pulsing with green heartbeats steady;
Forests thriving; oceans teeming – all ready.

For a dance divine, choreographed on Earth's grand stage,
Celebrating unity through every age.
It's here – between breaths taken wide,
That hope persists, eternally allied.

–

## Chorus United

Hear now the chorus united, a declaration bound tight,
Where Anthropocene whispers meld into Symbiocene light.
Each voice distinct, the young, the old – all who dwell,
Unite in purpose, their stories to tell.

From cloistered woods to urban sprawls aglow,
Every corner cultivated, compassionately grown.
Echoes building upon each day imbued,
As testament to attitudes renewed.

So, let these combined voices rise above,
The clamour of past wounds – to sing of love.
Proclaiming tales, not just of odysseys survived,
But of abundance thrived, as together we've strived.

–

## Anthropocene: A Verse Unfolding

Anthropocene: not a verdict but verse unfolding anew,
Seeds sown, sprouting through concrete into view.
Emerging landscapes transcend typical sights;
Sculpted by collective hands, pursuing lofty heights.

Thus, mankind marches towards horizons never seen,
Beneath the same stars that circle our sun's gleam.
An etched narrative ongoing, being spun
By threads of empathy, unwillingly undone.

Charting courses where dreams dare to merge with truth,
Into reality's embrace, wonderfully uncouth.
New chapters await an eager quill,
Poised to script the future, as only the poetic will.

—

## Harvest of Harmony – 8.4, 22:00

Beneath the sun's vigilant gaze, a harvest blooms – bold and bright,
A yield not of grain alone, but of humanity's conscious might.
Fields once fallow, now lush with myriad hues,
Share stories of revival, sprouted from care's dues.

This harmony harvested – a feast for soul and sense,
Evidence profound of collective resilience.
Gathered 'round tables extended across every divide,
Sharing sustenance where hope and purpose coincide.

In every kernel, a testament to unity sown,
Nurtured by waters from wisdom grown,
Roots delve deep into Earth's generous bosom, entwined,
Celebrating life in abundance intertwined.

–

## Tapestries Woven Wide

Across skies wide, tapestries woven thread by delicate thread,
Interlocking destinies shared, not outspread,
Of isolated journeys embarked in dread,
Revealing trails of communal bread instead.

Within these fabrics, eternal stories are told,
Patterns emerge, bold for both young and old.
Depicting scenes not solely crafted in gold,
But also shaded tales courageously extolled.

These textiles embrace each hand that weaves,
Recognizing contributions that interweave.
Crafting infinity, emblematic truths conceive,
Unified ambitions, in dreams we believe.

—

## Eclipse Transcended

Upon this canvas epoch-spun, an eclipse once shadowed is now transcended
By illuminations anew, our cosmos generously amended.
Darkness briefly cast – an invitation to appreciate,
The brilliance daylight gifts our estate.

Beyond mere luminescence perceived,
In cycles spun, Anthropocene grieved. Brighter constellations conceived,
Projecting pathways previously undeceived.

This light – a beacon guiding through time,
Guiding steps myriad, collectively climb.
Over mountains daunting, sublime,
Into valleys fruitful – into life's prime.

Anthropocene whispers no longer tales forlorn,
Bearing witness instead to Symbiocene dawn.
Each story's chapter, stanzas reborn,
Marking rhythm pulse, Earth sworn.

Thus the journey extends beyond vision known,
Unfolding an epic vast, deeply sown.
Bridging realms of the human heart, home,
Where understanding and love, universally grown.

–

## Gardeners of the Sky – 8.4, 22:02

In the gardeners' hands, where once lay dusk's grey hue,
Now dawn's palette, bright with promise, and ever true.
Caretakers not only of Earth beneath their feet,
But shepherds of the clouds and guardians of heat.

They sow seeds in skies – afore unseen –
Crafting weather patterns green;
A balance sought 'tween sunbeam and shadow cast,
Ensuring climates future-proofed and built to last.

With every cloud manicured, every storm gently tamed,
We rewrite the heavens with responsibility claimed.
A tapestry celestial, woven wide with care so fruitful,
Proclaims our role as stewards, rightfully and dutiful.

–

## Echoes of a New Age

Hear now – the echoes across oceans vast, transcending time:
Anthropocene's lessons morph into symphonies sublime.
These reverberations carry wisdom from tears shed prior,
Transforming grief into fuel for journeys higher.

Not just echoes but voices strong call forth an age reckoning:
Where human endeavours align under banners, awakening.
With nature's might harmoniously intertwined –
Portraits painted vividly by collective humankind.

Through these echoes, the past resonates anew, restored,
Laden with hope unlike any before explored:
Encouragements borne on winds previously stormed
Signalling epochs collaborative, commendably performed.

–

## The Compass Rose Redeemed

In latitude and longitude, bound by a compass rose so stately set,
Directions old assume meanings newly met.
North doesn't solely guide toward polar chill, nor south toward warmth to seek;
But inward towards conscience, bold yet meek.

Eastward lies innovation, sunrise kissed – aglow,
Westward reflects contemplation, a sunset's gentle show.
This compass redefined guides journeys, not on maps displayed,
But internal voyages through decisions weighed.

As navigators prudent within the Anthropocene rough sea survived,
Symbiocene shores ahead warmly contrived,
Through moral constellations, ethically derived,
Guiding humanities' ship, collectively revived.

–

## Epochs Transformed

From these verses, rich tapestries are drawn, life textured broad,
A remarkable epoch shift felt – a tactile nod,
Rendering past paradigms softly obsolete,
For horizon hopeful, feats brought to complete.

Within our grasp rests the capacity to transform, an active quake,
Reshaping futures tender, for fragile sake.
Marked by benevolence carved, a shared stake,
Upon a world cherished, our shared estate.

–

## Harmony's Horizon — 8.4, 22:03

Upon the cusp of day and night, where shadows merge with light,
A vision stands — harmony's horizon bright.
Here, contrasts fades into understanding deep,
Where once were divides, now rise bridges steep.

This newfound landscape breathes a sigh serene,
As if Earth herself had washed her face clean.
In every forest whisper, every river's roar,
Lies a melody of unity — forevermore.

The horizon calls not to distant lands unbound,
But to inward quests where true alignment's found.
O'er this horizon, humanity strides forth bold,
Crafting tales of the Symbiocene age, told.

—

## Voyagers of the Verdant Path

We are voyagers upon verdant paths unknown;
With every step taken, seeds of the future are sown.
Our compass lies within – the heart's sure guide;
Towards destinations where life is amplified.

These journeys, not solo but shared with kin
Of every form beneath nature's skin:
From the smallest ant to the towering tree,
All partake in this journey, wild and free.

Together we tread softly upon this Earth – revered;
Recognizing all that is cherished, endeared.
Upon green paths, our collective tales unfold,
Celebrating bonds that all enfold.

—

## Choirs Unseen

Amidst rustling leaves and whispers wind-borne,
Reside choirs unseen, in nature's grace adorned.
Their songs rise with cadence pure and true;
An overture for an audience too few.

Yet listen close – you'll hear their voices blend
With ours, as boundaries softly bend,
To reveal a chorus vast, joined by purpose linked,
Proliferation of hope from despair succinct.

A musical arrangement finely composed,
By hands both seen and unseen disposed,
Singing anthems strong enough to mend
Bruised hearts – an era newly penned.

—

## Anthems of Renewal

Through stanzas eternal, flow rivers of hope wild,
Leaving listeners moved, hearts undefiled.
Drawing together strings of destiny interwoven,
Marking days enlightened, with acts proven.

Thus unfolds the narrative: Anthropocene transposed
Into Symbiocene, in sonnet prose.
Recounting epochs' tale, continuously rising,
Buds burst open, a new dawn proposing.

—

## Reverie of the Regenerative – 9.4, 8:29

In landscapes painted with dawn's gentle hues,
Resides a dream – a reverie regenerative, true.
Where soil, once weary, breathes life anew,
Nourished by a bond 'twixt me and you.

Irresistible, grows this vision, verdant and wide,
Each step forward heals the divide.
Fields no longer idle, but lush with grain;
Forests echo with growth's refrain.

The age invites a pact to compose,
A future where every living being knows
Its value measured not in gold or gain,
But in harmony sustained – a collective refrain.

–

## Constellation of Caring

Above us sprawl constellations unknown,
Mapped not by light, but by love shown.
Stars named for empathy, shining bright –
Guiding through darkness with altruistic light.

This celestial embrace holds firm our course,
Towards an era where compassion is the force
That moves humanity beyond erstwhile divides,
Into realms where understanding abides.

Amidst these heavenly bodies vast,
Formed from actions kind – enduringly cast,
Lies proof that intentions pure, endure,
Considerate acts forever sure.

–

## Tomorrow's Tapestry Undone

Within each thread of tomorrow's tapestry – all colours unfurled, revealing
Vibrant potential held within Chronos' keepsake, ever concealing.
Yet threadbare moments demand delicate tending,
Re-weaving patterns towards horizons bending.

Not upon looms rigid, but fluid frames spanning,
Where warp meets weft – an encounter enchanting.
Together crafting scenes both grand and uplifting,
Dawning 'pon vistas continuously granting.

Thus, in our hands resides power profound,
To shape anew worlds from dreams unbound.
By nurturing seeds, latent hopes found,
Ensuring Symbiocene grounds will abound.

–

## Anthropocene to Symbiocene Transition

Anthropocene spawn now yield to Symbiocene's song,
A chorus engaged, ensuring the planet strong,
In union find solace, opposition long gone,
Embracing a shared fate for which hearts long.

Harmony crafted, where earnest desires belong,
Within an age where Earth and her children throng.
Nurtured into an era, neither short nor prolonged,
But timeless as nature's most resilient bond.

—

## Whispers in the Wilderness – 9.4, 8:45

In whispers shared between Earth and sky,
A tryst forms under nature's watchful eye.
Wilderness speaks in tones hushed yet profound,
Narrating tales of resilience, eternally wound.

Beneath canopies ancient, stories unfold,
Of symbiosis – true partnerships of old.
Within these murmurs, humanity finds,
A guide to living respectfully intertwined.

These whispers carry wisdom pure and sage,
Urging us towards a more enlightened age –
Where progress is measured not just by growth or expansion,
But by sustaining life's intricate tapestry – a collective intention.

–

## Dances with Dawn

Each daybreak brings dances with dawn anew,
A celebration of light, like the morning dew.
This dance – a reverent acknowledgment made
To the cycles that govern life's parade.

The sun rises – not as a solitary act,
But as part of an agreement intact;
An understanding that its warming rays
Feed the cycle supporting myriad ways.

Humanity joins this dance with open heart,
Integrating fully, without standing apart.
Moving to rhythms both ancient and ever new,
Recognising our role in keeping this balance true.

–

## Bridge Between Epochs

Between epochs lies a bridge carefully laid:
Stones carved from hope, with despair slowly unmade.
Across it walks humanity, wide-eyed and with care,
Treading lightly from Anthropocene bare into Symbiocene air.

Enriched by dreams Symbiocenic, an extended reach
Across divides – uniting past lessons with future strides.
Each step signifies a commitment keen
To mend what was hurt, to weave the unseen.

A fabric enveloping all in existence's tender embrace;
A holistic approach – all disparities to face.
Across this bridge, flows understanding deep,
As guardianship over Earth we seek to keep.

–

## In Times Transitioned

In times transitioned, ambition redefined,
Patterns emerge clearer, with destinies aligned.
Humanity stands, no longer merely resilient,
But transforms landscapes erstwhile silent.

Crafting echoes vibrant through acts consistent,
Ensuring a legacy vibrant, Symbiocene persistent.

—

## Canopy of Coalescence – 9.4, 9:03

Beneath a canopy where light and shadow dance,
The world come together – a confluence in trance.
Leaves whisper secrets, carried on the breeze:
A dialogue between beings, at ease.

This living ceiling, vast in its embrace,
Harbours tales of unity spanning time and space.
Here, humanity learns to listen and to understand –
Becoming part of something greater than grains of sand.

In this cathedral natural, born from Earth's own skin,
Lies proof that together we triumph, both within and kin.
Two worlds melding – one built, one wild –
Teaching each other to thrive, now reconciled.

–

## Ode to the Ocean's Song

To the ocean's endless song – a chorus deeply sown
Into the heartbeats of all lives known.
It sings of cycles, tides that rise and fall,
Reminding us we're part of something more – an inclusive call.

In waves that carry history to infinite sands,
Humanity finds guidance gently placed within its hands.
Learning rhythms ancient like the moon aloft – a binding spell
That connects every story we live to tell.

These waters vast hold both mystery profound,
And keys for continuance on common ground;
Urging us forward with wisdom saline-infused – a  soothing say:
"In connectedness lies strength," guiding our collective way.

–

## Summit's Silent Speech

Atop mountains' silent summits where Earth meets sky, expansive, wide,
We find our place within an orchestra so diverse it sparks inside;
An insight whispered windward – from craggy peak high overhead,
Compels us to a future of empathy instead.

From this elevated vantage point, clearly sees ambition redefined,
Not as dominion over land, but as stewardship kind;
Mountains speak not in words but reveal truths amplified:
Our potential is limitless when harmonised and aligned.

Thus, standing on these heights, gaze directed forth,
We embrace responsibility for all its sterling worth;
For from above, we see just how finite our sphere is,
Yet boundless are solutions when approached with clarity.

—

## Meadows of Mindfulness — 9.4, 9:05

Across the meadows of mindfulness, where thought flowers bloom,
Lies a simple realisation beneath grandeur and gloom.
Each blade of grass, each petal unique in its form,
Mirrors diversity's strength, thriving through the storm.

In this landscape serene, we wander with care,
Tending to ideas as seeds planted near.
Cultivating patience, understanding in turn —
From tending these fields, wisdom we learn.

Such expanses remind us: To pause is not to delay,
But to absorb deeper truths along the way.
Here humanity reconnects with Earth's subtle song —
A melody inviting all hearts to belong.

—

## Rivers Connective Flow

Rivers carve their paths with purpose, sure and slow,
Etching through landscapes with a unifying flow.
Their journeys winding from mountains down to sea,
Symbolizing life's connections between you and me.

These ribbons of water gather whispers from lands they pass;
Collecting tales of now, intertwined with shadows cast.
Flowing steadily forward without relent or rest,
Teaching us resilience; how to navigate our quests.

In their fluid cadence lies a potent truth decreed:
That unity is strongest when towards common goals we proceed.
Bearing lifeways diverse in each drop embraced,
Together forging futures too precious to be effaced.

—

## Symphony Reawakened

Upon an age's threshold where silence softly fades,
A symphony reawakens inside shadowy glades.
Notes carried forth by wind on leaves' quivering script,
Melodies harmonised effortlessly –
as though nature conspired and provided.

Instrumentation varied; each player vitally entwined,
To orchestrate convergence – not one left behind.
An ensemble collective, breathing mutual respect into day;
Harbingers of Symbiocene dawn – guiding our shared way.

Thus resounds music ancient yet never old:
Of coexistence brave, assertively bold.
A vibrant call across divides sown through time obscure;
The anthem for a future vibrantly pure.

–

## Gathering of the Guardians — 9.4, 9:21

In the grove where shadows merge with light's embrace,
A council gathers, guardians of this sacred space.
From distant corners of the Earth, their journey brings
Wisdom pooled from a wellspring pure – it sings.

They stand united in resolve and diverse creed,
Acknowledging each other's strengths through every deed.
Their vows not spoken but deeply felt within,
To protect life's tapestry – for all to begin anew.

This gathering speaks volumes without a word declared;
A promise made by actions, compassionate care shared.
For in their unity reflects humanity's hope, renewed,
To tend towards better futures where balance is pursued.

–

## Canvases Broadened

Upon canvases broadened beyond sight's grasp or mind's span,
Artistry unfolds in a collective plan.
Anchored not only in hues traditional or strokes bold,
But embracing changes vast, narratives untold,

These masterpieces display a richness so diverse,
Composing landscapes flourishing throughout our universe.
With each brush dipped into palettes newly found,
We draw borders erased and connections profound,

Revealing that beauty lies not solely in art displayed,
But also in expansive ways we've moved and swayed,
Together painting futures bright, inclusiveness conveyed;
On canvases broadened, together we've remained.

—

## Whispers Between Worlds

Between worlds seen and unseen, whisper secrets old;
Dialogues continuous and stories manifold.
The air vibrates with knowledge ancient, carried forth,
By winds with understanding of boundless worth.

In whispers soft between the terrestrial and divine,
Lies recognition mutual, crossing time.
Realms apart, connect in secrecy
By languages universal that align.

Hearing these messages requires a heart opened wide,
Tuned finely to frequencies on which wisdoms ride.
Listen close – Earth shares her guide,
In whispers between worlds, forever allied.

Acknowledging truths woven deep within drama vast;
Celebrating connections enduringly cast,
That ensures Symbiocene ideals robustly last,
Uniting everyone under nature's mast.

—

## Labyrinths of Legacy — 9.4, 9:22

Within the labyrinths where legacies entwine,
Paths meander, their patterns by design.
Here footsteps echo, tracing lines of fate —
Journeys charted by both small and great.

These corridors, that hold our histories dear,
Brim with tales of joy and fear.
Yet every turn within this maze intricate,
Leads us closer to a future we articulate.

For in these labyrinths of legacy profound,
The wisdom of ages past is found.
Guiding us through choices yet to make,
Ensuring we do not forsake for all life's sake.

—

## Echoes Across Eons

From ancient depths, where time's echoes resound,
A melody carries forth – a song profound.
It tells of epochs past, when Earth was young,
And speaks of futures still unsung.

Across eons vast, these reverberations span,
Connecting each woman, child, and man.
Reminding us that, though we may seem apart,
We share one Earth – it beats within our heart.

So heed these echoes, carried on the wind's wing;
Let them guide you – together they sing.
Harmonise your actions with nature's timeless tune,
To ensure tomorrow isn't met too soon.

–

## Gardens of the Mind

In gardens lush that bloom within the mind,
Thoughts grow wild, a tapestry intertwined.
Seeds sown from imagination take root,
Sprouting ideas brave; convictions absolute.

Watered by curiosity's gentle rain,
Nourished beneath knowledge's sunlit domain;
Blossoms unfurl — colours vivid against reason's grey
In these verdant fields where breakthroughs play,

Cultivate carefully this inner expanse wide,
Allow innovation and intuition to dance side-by-side.
Forests dense with insight, rather than wood,
Breathing life into dreams previously misunderstood.

Remember: in such gardens, thrive undeterred,
Solutions novel; voices yet unheard.
Fostering growth beyond mere words,
In minds' sanctuaries, inspiration spurred.

Embracing visions scribed across time, thick and thin,
Acknowledging interconnectedness, woven skin to -skin.
Humanity steps forward beneath a united banner high,
Where understanding is nurtured under a shared sky.

—

## Harvest of the Horizon – 9.4, 9:46

Upon horizons vast where dawn kisses night goodbye,
A convergence occurs 'neath the expansive sky.
This nexus, a harvest of light, dreams, and dew,
Promises beginnings adorned in hues anew.

Here, the seeds of tomorrow softly land,
Planted with care by time's tender hand.
Awaiting to sprout beneath sun's nurturing glare,
Yielding fruits born from unity's prayer.

In this place, potential lies awake,
In fields vast where choices are ours to make.
The horizon beckons, its breadth yet unknown;
A testament to how far collectively we've grown.

—

## Canopy of Unity

Above us stretches a canopy vast and grand,
Woven from threads spun across every land.
Its tapestry tells stories of triumph and trial,
Each stitch marks progress; each gap, a mile.

Under this sheltering presence, so wide,
Differences diminish with each stride.
Bound together under branches entwined –
A shared destiny for all humankind.

Beneath this arbour, shadows merge into light,
Symbols of peace over discord – day versus night.
Unity flourishes here – growth without end,
An inclusive embrace, our global message, we send.

–

## Rivers of Reflection

The rivers flowing gently mirror skies above,
Reflective surfaces whisper tales of love.
These waters meander through landscapes diverse,
Symbolizing lifelines unending and universe.

In their depths, wisdom ancient quietly resides:
Nature's secrets carried on eternal tides.
As currents shift, directions known not before,
They beckon us to explore – and then explore even more.

Leading us down paths reflective, deep within,
To discover connections beyond surface skin.
Encouraging introspection amidst life's din,
Revealing ties that bind – outside as well as in.
–
Thus unfolds a narrative, woven with intricate thread,
Of humanity's journey forward, brightly led.
Through labyrinthine path, unclearly seen,
Toward bright futures evergreen.

Within these tales, a significant braid is woven tight,
Echoing aspirations, a yearning for collective flight,
Towards reimagined realms, gained in sight,
Where harmonious coexistence stands affirmed as right.

–

### Summits of Serenity – 9.4, 9:56


Beyond the valleys where shadows play and
dance,
Lie summits bathed in tranquility's expanse.
Perched atop these pinnacles serene and stark,
Is a view unmarred by time's relentless mark.

This vantage point, high above the fray,
Offers perspective on the broader way.
Here, amidst stillness profound and rare,
Clarity emerges from thin alpine air.

These peaks whisper softly of strength quiet found
In moments of solitude where peace abounds.
Guiding us to appreciate life's grand scheme –
Reminding us that reality outstrips our dream.

—

## Oceans of Empathy

Oceans stretch wide with empathy's embrace,
Their waters deep cradle humanity's diverse face.
Each wave a gentle nudge towards understanding,
Carrying hopes and dreams, ever expanding.

Beneath these waves lie connections unseen –
Currents of what could be, not just what has been.
Together they surge forward, with purpose strong,
Encouraging each soul to sing its unique song.

In this expanse, so boundless and free,
Lies a blueprint for unity across land and sea.
Navigating storms or in sunlit calm days,
The ocean teaches resilience in countless ways.

–

## Grove of Gratitude

Within serenity's grove, where gratitude grows wild,
Nature offers lessons tender as a child.
Every leaf fluttering down speaks thanks;
Every root delving deep shares heartfelt ranks.

This sacred space, verdant, exists within reach,
A testament resilient, no adversity can breach.
Its bounty, limitless, provides sustenance more than food —
Fulfillment stemming from an attitude imbued.

Here, among whispers green where reflections are cast,
We find contentment intertwined vast;
Appreciating simple blessings amassed,
In the present moment — not lost to the past.
—
As narratives merge into fabric collectively wove,
Human endeavour glistening like treasure trove;
Echoes reverberate through halls, future shaped,
Encompassing ethos, compassion draped.

Through labyrinths navigated, heart lights guided,
Toward horizons envisioned, spirits ignited;
Our journey moves onward with resolve untied,
Humanity stands together, brightly lighted.

—

## Meadows of Melody – 9.4, 10:26

In meadows where melody and harmony converge,
Lies a symphony of life, vibrant and diverse.
Each blade of grass, a note within the score,
Sings with winds that dance across the moor.

This natural orchestra plays without end,
Reminding that breaks can mend, and hearts tend.
Its music flows, renewing spirits worn,
Birthing hope anew each songful morn.

Here, every creature's voice adds depth to the song –
Together in difference, inclusively belong.
The meadow's tune, a representation pure,
Of cohesion achieved when contrasts endure.

–

## Streams of Sanctuary

Flowing gently through valleys serene,
Streams carve sanctuaries in landscapes green.
Their waters whisper stories of resilience bold,
Narrating tales untold as ages unfold.

Within these banks lies a refuge sought by many –
Spaces sacred where burdens lighten aplenty.
Here, reflections deepen beyond surface gleam,
Unlocking wisdom from nature's dream.

These streams nurture not just land but soul,
Guiding us toward a collective goal:
To find peace amidst life's hurried pace,
In water's gentle embrace – sanctuary's grace.

—

# Constellations of Connection

Starlit skies reveal constellations bright,
Patterns illuminating connections light.
Across vast expanses, this celestial map
Links individuals into unity's lap.

Such configurations mirror bonds on Earth –
Weaving humanity together since birth.
Though stars may seem far apart and separate,
Interconnectedness remains at heart's gate.

These starry guides remind us, night by night;
That unity is forged even out of sight.
Reflecting beneath constellations spread wide,
Is our journey – walking in nations side by side.

Through narratives intertwining like vines grow,
From whispers windborne to ocean depths below.
A tapestry emerges, complex yet clear,
Celebrating ties woven dear.

Bridging divisions, fear once sowed,
Cherishing moments where kinship flowed,
Onward strides humanity's glow,
Guided by compassion's endless tow.

—

## Canopy of Compassion – 9.4, 11:35

Beneath the expansive canopy where compassion lays,
Every leaf, every branch interlays.
A shelter formed from empathy's embrace,
Casting shadows of solace across Earth's face.

This living dome, so verdant and vast,
Echoes with kindnesses from the past.
Here, humanity finds refuge and rest,
In the gentle fold of nature's best.

For within this canopy high above ground,
Unity and love are profoundly found.
Resonating through its leaves with every breeze,
Are whispers of peace among the trees.

Such a sanctuary offers not just shade but light,
Guiding us towards what is truly right:
To live in harmony under shared skies,
Where compassion grows strong and never dies.

—

## Gardens of Generosity

Gardens where generosity blooms wild and free,
Showcase abundance meant for you and me.
Each fruit, each flower – a gift to share,
Rooted deeply in soil tended with care.

These gardens extend beyond mere plots of land;
They flourish in hearts willing to understand
That true wealth lies not in hoarding seed,
But in nurturing growth among those in need.

From these generous grounds springs forth a force robust:
A commitment to ensure no one is left in the dust.
Here, our harvests feed more than physical hunger –
Fulfilling souls, starved for kindness, no longer.

Amidst such bounty, realised through collective deed,
We discover fulfillment surpassing greed.
Blooming brightly – the essence indeed
Of living fully is sowing that generous seed.

–

## Rivers of Resolve

Resolve flows like rivers, mighty and profound –
Through landscapes varied, it covers ground.
Persistent in its journey against all odds faced;
It carves routes new – obstacles embraced.

These waters surging symbolise mankind's will,
Bending neither to complacency nor struggles uphill.
Driven by currents deep within our core,
Never stagnant; always seeking more.

Within their depths lies strength untold,
Power harnessed as bold tales unfold.
Reflecting resolve resolute, in relentless chase,
Shaping futures bright as water pass with grace.

Thus, do these timeless streams continuously refine
Our collective resolve, along a grand design.
Flowing forward, united by a singular mind,
Towards horizon ahead, together aligned.

–

## Auroras of Aspiration – 9.4, 13:35

On the night's canvas, aspirations paint their hue,
Auroras dance vibrant on a backdrop of velvet blue.
These lights – nature's poetry in motion, true,
Speak to dreams unfettered and visions ever new.

Gleaming across polar skies with stories untold,
Each shimmer signifies hopes made bold.
An atmospheric reminder that even in the darkest night,
Ambition lift us, guided by an inner light.

Spectacles ethereal remind all who gaze below,
Of the limitless potential human hearts bestow.
Under this celestial ballet of glow, majestic so,
We unite beneath aspiration's brilliant echo.

–

## Summits of Synergy

Where mountain peaks meet the infinite sky,
Stands synergy – the summit where efforts collide.
Not a collision harsh, but a merging soft as dawn's first light;
Efforts combined,  burdens lifted, making challenges slight.

This peak doesn't stand alone, uniquely high –
It is among ranges where our potentials lie.
Climbing together, through trials, stone by stone,
Reaching heights not possible alone.

Here, at altitude removed from solitary fight,
Shared vision clears, like stars bright in the night.
From these summits, we gain perspective profound;
Where unity fosters strength that truly abounds.

–

## Orchards of Opportunity

Stretching far under sunlit skies so clear,
Lie orchards ripe with opportunity dear.
Trees heavy with fruits yet to be tasted,
Root in soil rich, ensuring nothing is wasted.

Each seed sown in anticipation great,
Promises blooms for those willing to partake.
Branches bending under possibilities' weight;
Offering opportunity anew to create.

This fertile place nurtures what tomorrow brings;
Nourished by effort, where tended promises spring.
Here, amidst rows endless, hope sings,
For hands ready to reap what diligent toil rings.

Walking through these fields, in abundance we bask,
In shared commitment to growth – an unspoken task.
Bound by a belief strong, never asked,
That together our lives are more plentiful, unmasked.

Through narratives varied, connecting dot-to-dot,
Adventurous spirits find conspiracies, bemusing and fraught.
Guided wandering, seeking what is sought,
Setting sail on winds caught, toward futures thought.

–

## Harbour of Hearts – 9.4, 13:39

In the harbour where hearts in repose dock,
A gentle swaying brings serenity's clock.
Amidst waters calm and embracing wide,
Lie connections robust, that through storms abide.

This port, a testament to unity's might,
Illuminated by understanding's soft light.
Anchors dropped deep within compassion's well,
Hold vessels steady against tides that swell.

In this refuge benevolent, where spirits meld,
Every pulse, each urge is here upheld.
For in this haven, diversity finds rest,
Proving once more, that together we're at our best.

–

# Canvases of Constancy

Across canvases broad, impossibly grand,
Constancy paints with a meticulous hand.
With strokes deliberate that time cannot erode.
It crafts landscapes where loyalty showed.

Each hue chosen speaks of unwavering themes,
Commitment flows in each scene it deems.
Through fields golden, ripe with confidence grown wild,
To oceans azure, deep with promises compiled.

These works of art stand firm, unswayed,
Monuments to devotion freshly laid;
Reflecting bonds resiliently displayed
On canvases eternal – where love's never frayed.

–

## Tomorrows Tethered Together

From the loom of destiny, tomorrows are spun,
Tethered together under the same sun.
Interwoven threads – diverse yet akin:
Compose a tapestry of what could have been,

But also what is – an existence shared;
By trials multiplied but equally bared.
Together facing forward – we venture bold,
Collectively crafting futures untold.

The weave dense with aspirations found;
Encounters many – a life richly wound.
Thus, we journey on – a single thread,
Bound in hope's vibrant quilt spread ahead.

Humanity dances on thread-lines fine,
Spanning horizons where dreams intertwine.
With hands joined across divides by design,
We navigate realms time tried to redefine.

Anchored not by past solemn shrine,
But propelled by visions upon which we dine,
Feasting on futures aligned,
In worlds reimagined, boundlessly entwined.

—

## Gardens of Gestures – 9.4, 13:43

Beneath the canopy of common skies, gardens flourish, tender and wise,
Rooted in acts small yet profound, it's here kindness never dies.
Each gesture a seed sown deep with care,
Sprouting into deeds, fair beyond compare.

These are the fields where empathy blooms bright,
Nourishing souls through nurturing light.
A harvest rich with giving hands unfurled –
Gestures cultivating goodness in the world.

In each blossom, whispers tales untold –
Of warmth amid days dark and cold.
Through such gardens strides humanity's best gait:
Where giving becomes our natural state.

–

## Lanterns of Legacy

Lanterns hanging high – legacy's guiding flare –
Casting lights that travel far, connecting here to there.
Glowing resolutely through night's deepest despair,
Serving as beacons for those seeking solace rare.

Each lantern a testament to paths travelled wide,
Illuminating footsteps where hopes reside.
Around such lights, stories gather diverse and rife,
Celebrating legacies laden with life.

In their gentle glow, we find reflections clear:
The enduring power of connections held dear.
Beneath legacy's illuminated bower,
Humanity finds strength united – a force empowered.

–

## Streams Converging

Confluence marks where converging streams blend,
Uniting waters separate toward a common end.
Here, currents mingle – their voices sing,
Of bond formed strong; an interconnected spring.

From divergent sources, these waters arise,
Journeying forth under shared skies;
Their merging signifies more than meets the eye:
A union signaling unity ever nigh.

Such is humanity's ceaseless quest:
To find in each other kinship expressed.
Resembling streams which together flow,
Bound by ties that steadfast grow.

Through metaphors vivid, painted on time's span,
We witness not just artistry but destiny of man.
Crafted hour by hour with a delicate hand –
Each metaphor a strand, woven grand.

Linking us all through this land,
In unity bound by nature's band,
Revealing potential, wonderfully planned,
In every heart, across sea and sand.

—

## Symphony of Solidarity – 9.4, 13:49

In the world's great orchestra, each soul finds its part,
Playing melodies of solidarity that stem from the heart.
With instruments varied, tunes both new and old,
Together they create a symphony bold.

Strings vibrate with compassion in melodious plea,
Woodwinds whisper of freedom, soaring high and free.
Percussion pounds out justice – rhythms strong and clear,
Brass blares triumphant hope, trumpeting far and near.

This ensemble united under humanity's grand score,
Proclaims unity's power louder than ever before.
In this harmony lies strength rare:
A world together standing – an anthem of care.

—

## Atlas of Affinity

Upon this atlas spread wide – a cartography exquisite:
Maps not of lands apart, but of hearts intimately knit.
Contours drawn not by distance, but by emotion felt;
Marking territories where understanding deep dwells.

Rivers here flow not to seas, but into souls converge,
Mountains rise as challenges we together surmount;
Forests vast – a canopy under which diversity emerges,
Deserts bloom – with resilience springs an eternal fount.

Such is the geography of our shared sphere,
Traversed by bridges made from stories sincere.
Across this atlas boundless, affinity shows:
Where empathy plants its seed, kinship grows.

—

### Voyagers of Vision – 9.4, 14:43

Across horizons endless, where dreams are set sail,
Voyagers of vision embark without fail.
With compasses crafted from hope and resolve,
Charting courses daring, mysteries to solve.

Their vessels powered by a collective quest for light,
Navigating seas of ignorance, dark as night.
Crews diverse in thought, yet united in aim,
Seeking shores untarnished by prejudice or blame.

In this odyssey vast, each star a guiding tale,
Illuminating paths where courage must prevail.
Together they journey toward understanding's dawn –
A testament to what can be when hearts are drawn.

—

## Tapestries Twined Tight

In the grand hall of humanity's woven fate,
Tapestries twined tight with threads ornate.
Each fiber a deed, every colour a creed,
Interweaving stories upon which our futures feed.

Here patterns emerge from chaos contained,
Revealing images richly framed;
Histories etched into weave so fine –
Silent testaments to the passage of time.

But look closer still at the spaces between:
Gaps filled with opportunities yet unseen.
For it's in the interstices that light shines,
Promising revisions designed by hands divine.

–

## Chorus Celestial Claimed

Beyond Earth's embrace, under celestial awning wide,
A chorus amongst stars subtly implied.
Voices not bound by gravity's chain,
Singing songs sweet of joy and pain.

This ethereal chorus, tied by cosmic bonds,
Echoes harmony that eternally responds;
Carried across voids silent and deep –
Lullabies the universe promises to keep.

Such is the music we're destined to join one day,
Human voices blending amidst the astral ballet.
A chorus celestial claimed – spirits intertwined,
In stardust melodies eternally aligned.

–

## Dawns of Discovery – 9.4, 14:49

Each sunrise heralds a dawn of discovery, where light cascades,
Illuminating paths through the shadowy glades.
With every ray that breaks the night's embrace,
Reveals a world aglow with wonder and grace.

In this perpetual unveiling, eyes wide in awe,
Behold landscapes transformed, without flaw.
Horizons expand as knowledge takes flight –
An endless quest in pursuit of insight.

Here, in these moments so fleetingly held,
Reside possibilities, by curiosity swelled.
A canvas awaiting strokes bold and new,
Dawning discoveries fresh as the morning dew.

–

## Whispers of Wisdom

Beneath canopies ancient, whispers weave through still air,
Carrying wisdom profound that time cannot impair.
Leaves rustle with secrets of ages gone by,
Urging souls to listen closely, and aim high.

These murmurs soft are nature's gentle guide,
Offering counsel no heart can deride.
Through countless cycles, they have watched empires rise and fall,
Standing as a testament to resilience through it all.

Heed these words, not spoken but felt deep within –
Echoes reminding us of where we've been.
And hinting subtly at what might be achieved,
When whispered wisdom is fully conceived.

–

## Globes of Grace

Our globe spins gracefully on an axis unseen —
A celestial dance amidst void's vast sheen.
Orbiting a life giving warmth unfurled,
Graciously moving in a world vast, pearled.

This sphere — a mosaic wondrously made:
From snowy caps, white, to jungles' rich shade;
Oceans azure deep, breathing rhythm slow —
All intricately connected below.

In this rotation lies a cryptic code;
For living beings together intimately abode.
Reminding us daily as east greets west,
That grace surrounds us when we pause and rest.
 —
In composed verse or unwritten law we abide,
Stories told beneath the cosmic tide.
Human experience — a rivulet wide,
Through galaxies untamed, does glide.

Amidst the Universal Symphony, alongside challenge, we stride,
As voyagers eternal, with infinite worlds implied.
Discover anew realms that simply hide,
In explorations shared, with united pride.

 —

## Seasons of Serendipity – 9.4, 14:55

Upon the wheel of time, seasons turn in serendips play,
Gifting moments unexpected in their display.
Each cycle, a tapestry woven tight with fate's hand,
Revealing beauty unintended, intricately across the land.

In spring's bloom or winter's cold embrace,
Lies hidden serendips, encased in place.
For within every change – a chance anew
To find wonder in perspectives shifted into view.

As seasons cycle with graceful ease,
We're reminded of life's unplanned harmonies.
Embracing each transformation, bold and free –
Finding joy in what is, and in what might be.

–

~~~

# THE LEGACY OF RENEWAL

## The Legacy of Renewal – 10.4, 13:21

In gardens where humanity's shadow once loomed large,
New growth emerges through cracked concrete – resilient, resolute.
Life, persistent always, sprawls beyond barriers set by our own hands;
This verdant testament stands as symbol and substance of regeneration –
A legacy reforged in the crucible of necessity.

Amidst lands scarred by extraction and neglect,
Revitalization unfolds under stewardship renewed;
Where once was depletion, now thrives collaboration –
A symbiosis of mankind and nature, meticulously curated.
Our footprints, mindful and lighter, tread paths of reparation,
Strengthening ties with ecosystems once deemed inexhaustible.

–

## Anthropic Catalysts

Innovation flourishes from pressing need – the Anthropocene compels;
Technological marvels, born from desperation, shine as beacons:
Carbon captured from air, turned artefact or fuel,
Oceans cleansed as inventions draw poison out like venom.
Farmers, guardians at biodiversity's frontier, usher in a new era,
Where agriculture heals as it feeds.

Education evolves, embracing this grand narrative –
Instilling virtues of humility before forces ancient,
While respecting human agency within ecological spheres.
Young minds, ignited with purpose and deeply rooted in interconnectedness –
Carry forth the torch lit from crisis-stoked embers.

As this story unfolds on global stages, both vast and intimate,
The essence is not mere survival, but flourishing.
It reveals latent capacities, untapped potentials –
Divining water deep beneath deserts now made lush.
Within reach lies not only averting collapse,
But cultivating an age revered for wisdom gleaned in dark times,
Now brought into light.

An epoch of renewal, rather than ruin, beckons –
Charged with ensuring Closing Time is temporal, relegated to narratives past,
Replaced with a future inscribed in vibrant hues of hope.
Determination collective proves humanity's capacity to transcend itself,
Remaking the world into a sanctuary,
Where life diverse harmonises, in a chorus echoed through eternity.

–

## Nebulae of Dreams

Deep within cosmic seas where darkness reigns supreme,
Nebulae form from stardust – incubators of dreams.
These celestial nurseries, vibrant and vast,
Craft futures untold, visions recast.

Here, stars are born from chaos' gentle hold,
Illuminating mysteries eternally retold.
Through astral whispers, dreams take flight,
Crossing void dimensions towards hope so bright.

Gaze upon night skies, dark yet profound –
Realise there, our aspirations are found.
Woven within cosmos' grand, sweeping scheme,
Are endless possibilities yet to gleam.

–

## Harmonics of Heritage

Our world resonates with harmonics rich – an heritage agelessly endured.
Echoes bound through canyons storied, by countless cultures secured.
Each rhythm found under sun-kissed skies or moonlit chimes,
Speaks of a legacy enduring beyond the confines of time.

These sounds form an orchestra, ancestral and profound;
Each note a memory, every melody a resonant sound.
Binding us together – past and present intertwined,
Clarifying we are but strands in history's refined weave.

Listen closely when silence falls as dusk's light wanes:
Amidst quietude, ancient wisdom reigns.
Inheritances shared through whispers, breaths transpired,
Ensure stories of old ignite sparks anew, endlessly inspired.

Universality claims not just space explored afar,
But also depths within – revealing who we truly are.
Engaging dialogues 'tween now and a shared star,
We find our collective identity beneath a luminous avatar.

–

## Arcadia of Affection

In lush Arcadia, where affections flows,
The heart finds its echo in everything aglow.
A realm where compassion paints every hill and dale;
Kindness weaves through each tale, a wind-filled sail.

This idyllic space, vibrant with connection's bloom,
Offers sanctuary from the world's prevailing gloom.
Here, every stranger finds not just a friend,
But tales of division gracefully come to an end.

In Arcadia's warm embrace, souls deeply intertwine,
With strings unseen – a purposeful design;
Uniting all in mutual respect, so dearly revered,
An emblem to which open hearts are securely moored.

–

## Odyssey of Oneness

Upon life's vast ocean, where currents are strong,
Sails an odyssey where all belong.
A voyage under stars' watchful lights,
Guided by oneness — not divides nor petty fights.

This journey charts a constellation course wide,
Not for a single sailor, but for a shared ride.
Collaborative quests beneath a universal dome,
Proving Earth is not just a place, but our home.

En route, discoveries manifold unfold:
That unity fosters strengths, untold.
Harmony prevails as divisive waves abate,
Upon this enlightened voyage, we find our state.

—

## Beacons Beyond Boundaries

Across horizons wide, beacons boldly shine;
Signals piercing barriers once defined.
Each luminary's cast dispels the land of shadows,
Extending an invitation – to understand, to know.

Beyond mere boundaries etched by hand or word;
Where voices varied  are collectively heard.
Around these beacons, common ground is found,
Where shared humanity is fundamentally sound.

Illuminating fellowship beyond geographic confines,
Revealing how diversity truly defines and shines.
Luminous beacons signal compassionate signs,
Joining distant corners through bonds entwines.

From verses whimsical to proclamations profound,
Humanity's saga continues, bound,
In exploration both inward and outward found.
Along paths pantomimed, possibilities abound.

Navigating the spectrum of myriad encounters,
Realizing a cosmos connected, a  backdrop that astounds.
Acknowledging amidst diversity, peace resounds,
Celebrating our oneness, a connection profound.

—

## Symphony of Sentience

In the grand orchestra where every life plays,
A symphony of sentience beautifully conveys.
Notes high and low, in harmony engaged,
Illustrating connections across epochs, pages aged.

This collective melody, resonant and deep,
Echoes a promise of unity for us to keep.
From the tiniest ant to the towering tree that sways,
Each contributes their voice to these endless days.

Such music pulses with vitality pure,
Encouraging hearts towards empathy, sure and secure.
In this orchestration vast, a truth profound gleams:
In shared existence lies the most deepest theme.

—

## Atlas of Awe

Upon sprawling pages, an atlas wide unfolds,
An odyssey inked in awe each chapter boldly holds.
Here be dragons no more; instead, wonder reigns,
Mapping out terrains boundless curiosity contains.

Each compass swing reveals more than just directions;
But paths leading toward introspection's connections.
Beyond mere borderlines or contours that delineate,
Woven threads of fate, invite us to relate and contemplate.

Journey through this atlas, eyes alight with glee,
For it charts not just lands but humanity's vast sea.
Across its expanse, discover tales both tall and true;
Realizing awe is found not just looking outward – but within too.

—

## Gardens of Genesis

Amidst verdant gardens beneath Genesis skies anew –
Where seeds sprout stories old, rephrased, renewed.
Blooms abound, potential rich in nectar's drape,
Rooted deep in Earth's nurturing scape.

This living mosaic, crafted by hands both meek and bold,
Celebrates cycles undying, ever unrolled.
Showcasing diversity unparalleled, stories boldly told;
A boundless tapestry, nature's artistry, perfectly enfolded.

These fertile grounds declare loudly life's enduring song,
Echoing a principle cherished long:
That beginnings spring eternal, where they belong,
In gardens where life's threads weave strong and throng.

Through prose poetic or silent, a steadfast gaze,
To wonders manifold, drawn near in a daze,
We unveil continuity in realms both near and far,
An anthology universal, where all stories are.

Humanity strides forth as pioneer,
'Neath a canvas celestial – sheer and sincere.
Vision expanding, sphere by sphere,
Embracing all, free from doubt or fear.

—

## Luminaries of Lore

Amidst the vast tapestry where stories intertwine,
Stand the Luminaries of Lore, human and divine.
Guardians of wisdom from ages long past,
Bearing tales where shadows are cast.

These bearers of light illuminate paths once dim,
Guiding souls through history's whim.
Their legacy shines, a beacon for all to see,
A shared heritage binding you and me.

In their radiant glow, we find strength to forge ahead,
Carrying the lessons of those long dead.
Through misty veils of time, their voices carry,
Echoes that guide us, ensuring we never tarry.

—

## Canvases Unbound

Upon canvases unbound, spread endless hues,
Each stroke a testament to myriad views.
Here, artistry and possibility freely blend,
Crafting realities that beautifully transcend.

This landscape wide invites exploration deep,
Encouraging dreamers, awake or asleep.
No borders confine imagination's flight;
Every colour dances delightfully in light.

Such boundlessness inspires creation anew,
Offering perspectives fresh as morning dew.
Within this artful domain, arises visions clear:
Opportunity unlimited, unfettered by fear.

—

## Rhapsody in Resonance

A rhapsody resounds through ether's space;
A melodic resonance uniting the human race.
Its harmony speaks not just in sound decibels loud,
But whispers quietly in unity proud.

This symphony celebrates diversity's span —
Each note part of an elaborate plan.
Together they create music deeply profound,
Transcending barriers, without a single bound.

Engage with this rhapsody; let its melody unfold,
Fostering connections that are ages old.
Within resonance, found between heartbeats syncopated;
Lies understanding, universally stated.

Embarking on sojourns, weaving narratives intricate,
Navigating interstellar connections to negotiate.
Humanity's chorus — voices variate,
Composes a universal anthem, cultivating fate.

In convergence, cosmic destinies illustrate,
Via harmonic chords, we oscillate.
Humanity united, resonating,
Upon a journey, reinvigorating.

—

## Oasis of Origins

Within the heart lies an oasis deep,
A sanctum where core essences sleep.
In silence profound and innate connections,
Reside truths fundamental, inviting reflections.

This inner haven, untouched by outer din,
Harbours seeds of potential for those who seek within.
A wellspring of origins, pure in form and intent,
Nurturing self-awareness and enlightenment.

In this tranquil refuge, away from time's relentless chase,
We discover our beginnings – a universal base.
From this point of inception, so clear and so bright,
Emerge paths divergent, bathed in light.

–

## Voyage Through Veils

Upon the vessel named Curiosity, we sail with zest,
Through veils that separate our quest.
These ethereal barriers part at inspired touch,
Revealing realms unseen, desired much.

Our trajectory arcs towards wonders liminal;
Transient borders dissolve, thresholds minimal.
Between complacency known and mysteries uncharted,
Lies adventure abundant – in pursuit, recompense imparted.

Onward we sail through veils diaphanous, sheer,
Embracing novel horizons, drawn ever near.
Each journey transcends mere geographic bounds;
Exploring territories where revelation resounds.

–

## Concordance Crescendo

All elements converge in a concert sublime,
Crafting out of chaos a rhythm divine.
Air, Earth, water – even fire's fierce embrace,
Unite under nature's grace.

This concordance crescendo heralds an awakening grand,
A resonant call that sweeps from sea to land.
Uniting disparate beings, drawn nigh
Under a common sky, infinitely high.

Nature orchestrates with a hand unseen,
A symphony vibrant on life's stage serene.
Harmonies blended, perfectly attuned,
Heralding a peace soon promised.

In narratives woven with complexity and grace,
Humanity ventures forth – space to space.
Discovering links, an inseparable thread,
Crafting a tapestry united, where diversity is celebrated.

A journey shared, a collective race,
Towards harmony's tender, all-encompassing place.
Echoes of unity carry forward, a timeless base,
In humanity's enduring, interstellar embrace.

–

## Globes of Gratitude

Encircled in the warm glow of gratitude's light,
Worlds within and beyond pulse with vibrant might.
In every thank-you whispered, every act so kind,
A globe spins – a testament to the ties that bind.

These globes, illuminated by kindness's soft rays,
Shimmer through even the darkest days.
Casting long shadows of joy unbridled,
Celebrating connections gained and sustained.

Through these orbs, deep feelings dance,
About reverberations of benevolence.
Gratitude's gravity draws hearts near,
Uniting us all in a cosmos clear.

–

## Streams of Serenity

Streams of serenity, flow gently, through life's varied terrain,
Carrying calm where once stood strife and pain.
These clear waters mirror skies so vast,
Reflecting moments – present, future, past.

Along their banks, flowers untouched by worry, grow,
Unhurried they flourish , bathed in tranquility's glow.
Creatures great and small take a sip –
Finding solace beside waters deep.

May we find such streams when weary we become,
And drink deeply from peace, with welcome.
Let its currents guide our thoughts to a gentle eddy –
In stillness deep, may we be ready.

–

## Anthems Ardent

From deepest valleys to the highest peak,
Voices rise – an anthem seekers speak.
With verses strong, born of passion, true,
Telling tales, old yet ever new.

This song – a chorus collectively sings,
Of dreams envisioned on hope's broad wings.
United notes carried far on wind's back,
Spanning divides, leaving no lone track.

Such is humanity's ardent hymn:
A shared endeavour; beyond mere whim.
Together crafting a world reimagined,
Where love for all is zealously enshrined.

Crafted amidst trials and tribulations, proud,
Humanity stands – together, loud.
On a journey personal, in a collective shroud,
Discoveries anew, courage avowed.

Echoes across the cosmos – a recognition vowed,
In unity, our strength unequivocally endowed.
Guiding principles shared, culturally allowed,
Cultivating spaces where understanding is ploughed.

–

## Wellsprings of Wisdom

Across the vast expanse where knowledge flows,
Lie wellsprings deep, where wisdom grows.
In serene repose, secrets are unveiled,
Offering guidance through mists once assailed.

Drink deeply from these springs, pure and clear,
Quenching the thirst for understanding dear.
Each drop carries tales from eras gone by,
With insights profound, that never will die.

In wisdom's embrace, find solace and strength,
Navigating life's breadth and length.
For within its depths lie answers sought long,
Harmony's notes in life's complex song.

—

## Bridges of Benevolence

Spanning wide rivers and chasms steep,
Are bridges built strong, with foundations deep.
Crafted from kindness, compassion, and care,
They connect disparate shores everywhere.

Walking these pathways, bound by pledges true,
Bringing distant hearts into view.
A testament to humanity's enduring grace,
Against tides divisive, they firmly brace.

So let us tread lightly on each span designed
By love's architects with unity in mind.
Building more bridges across rifts we find,
Joining all people – heart, soul, combined.

—

## Orbitals of Optimism

In the celestial dance where hope holds sway,
Orbitals bright light our way.
Planets aligned under optimism's glow,
Guide us through life's ebb and flow.

These cosmic paths chart journeys that soar high,
Above shadows cast on the world below.
Emboldened by faith in a bright tomorrow,
Our spirits take flight 'neath stars alight.

Embrace the vast, expansive universe's spin,
Through galaxies dark and astir within.
Let every orbital your heart claims
Illuminate your life with fervent flames.

Each narrative strand weaves a tapestry fine,
Through verses spoken, line by line.
Humanity forward leans, intertwined
With the grand cosmic design aligned.

Stitched together, is our cultural rind,
Upon a canvas infinite, design unsigned.
Poems eternal and minds entwined,
Echo through time, in mankind.

—

## Harbours of Harmony

In tranquil bays where currents meet and merge,
Lie harbours safe, a refuge from life's surge.
Here sails are furled, and anchors cast deep,
In waters calm, reflecting skies vast and steep.

These havens, hushed by serenity's embrace,
Are ports where weary souls find peace and grace.
A gathering of vessels, diverse yet akin –
United in their quest for solace within.

Within each harbour, protective arms extend,
New melodies of harmony begin to blend.
Resonating with the rhythm of shared dreams,
Fostering a unity that truly redeems.

–

## Starscapes of Solidarity

Beneath night's velvet dome, where starscape sprawls,
We stand connected – a cosm in awe recalls.
Each star, a beacon across the infinite black,
Symbolises unity; no celestial body lacks.

This firmament vast, an expanse bridging all divides,
Under which every seeker eventually abides.
Gazing upwards, our differences fade to naught;
Bound by wonder, solidarity is sought.

Let these constellations be our guiding creed;
Routes mapped not by division, but mutual need.
Across galaxies wide or earthly realm beside,
In solidarity's starscape, forever shall we abide.

–

## Gardens Growing Gratitude

Through verdant realms where gratitude takes seed,
And blossoms forth in actions kind, indeed,
Lies gardens growing rich beneath love's light,
Offering sustenance, through day and night.

Rooted deep, this thankfulness blooms,
Inviting more than mere floral perfumes.
It nurtures the soul's soil – transforming gloom,
Into spaces vibrant, where hope can resume.

Tending these grounds with gentle hands,
We reap harvests far beyond mere lands.
In gratitude's garden we understand,
The bounty held when hearts expand.

Each step forward on this journey is marked
By crossings significant, underscored stark.
Intertwined melodies harmonically embark
On odysseys bold where humanity sparks.

Reflecting on chords collective, plucked so dark,
Revealing auroras over landmarks that hark –
Resonating a chorus of unity, illuminating an arc,
Guiding us through life's journey like a celestial lark.

–

## Canopy of Constellations

Under a canopy woven with constellations bright,
Where starlight drapes the tranquil cloak of night.
Amidst the cosmos' silent symphony, serene,
Lies a connection boundless – seen and unseen.

This celestial mantle, vast beyond measure,
Holds tales ancient and moments current – a treasure.
Guided by its patterns, navigators, old and new,
Find direction in its expanse so true.

Beneath this astral cover spreads a sense profound,
Of oneness as vast as the skies abound.
Stars shimmer not only with light, but with hope's gleam,
Binding us all in this universal dream.

–

## Meadow of Metamorphosis

In meadows where change flows free as the air,
Transformation unfurls with grace rare.
Butterflies emerge under the sun's gentle kiss –
A testament to nature's cyclical bliss.

Each petal, every leaf in these fields wide,
Echoes life's perennial urge to coincide
With rhythms both ancient yet ever new,
Crafting landscapes vibrant with every hue.

Such meadowlands are monument and guide:
To grow through change is to live a life amplified.
Amidst metamorphoses, grand or subtly detected –
One finds resilience – an honour to be reflected.

–

## Rivers of Reflection

Navigating rivers flowing deep through time's embrace,
Carrying currents rich with history's trace.
Their waters mirror skies above so high —
An everlasting dialogue 'twixt Earth and sky.

Upon these banks, where contemplation finds its space,
Streams flow unwavering, past collides with future face.
Blending into one course — reflections on existence —
A silent force persistent.

Whether babbling brooks or mighty tides sweeping wide,
These waterways carry lessons profound inside.
Reminding us that life's ever-revolving slide
Is mirrored in their journey — a reflective guide.

Through prose painted vivid, shared dreams ignite,
Humanity ventures into depths with insight.
Embracing connections, unscathed by slight,
Resonating across vastness, bridging the night.

Upon such narratives, born aloft in spirited flight,
Crafted fine from collective sight — we unite.
Endeavour bold beneath starscape light,
Journeys intertwine, forging bonds tight.

—

## Vistas of Virtue

Across sprawling vistas where dawn's light softly lands,
Lies a testament to virtues held in open hands.
Horizons wide with promise, reveal path and purpose clear,
Guiding sojourners forward, beyond the realm of fear.

In valleys green and mountains grand, virtues alike endure,
Echoing integrity, courage, love – in their strike, all pure.
These landscapes vast are not merely terrains to traverse,
But realms where strong hearts thrive, casting blessings diverse.

Within nature's cathedral, under a canopy sky-spanned,
We witness noble deeds unfold across the land.
Each action taken – a cornerstone laid –
Building foundations strong, where virtues remain claimed.

–

## Aurora of Alliance

Beneath auroras dancing bright 'cross polar night's expanse,
Shimmers an alliance profound, born not by chance.
Colours blend seamlessly on a celestial canvas stretched wide,
Portraying unified hope that forever shall abide.

This spectral ballet weaves bonds unseen yet deep felt,
A reminder that together, promises are better kept,
Stronger than alone, shared dreams take flight,
Pushing back the darkness with collective light.

Such are the ties fostered under glowing skies,
Emerging as beacons where our strength lies.
Proclaiming solidarity for ages, hence inscribed
By bold strokes in the sky, vividly described.

—

## Atelier of Aspirations

In this atelier, aspirations soar,
Ideas spread their wings, gracing every door.
Here, creation never tarnishes or fades into grey –
Instead, it blooms vibrant – displaying artistry's full array.

Minds mingle, talents weave threads of gold,
Crafting brilliant futures from ancient moulds.
Ambitions painted on canvases stretched taut –
Desires sculpted fine, with passion caught.

In a studio boundless – an imagination's forge;
Where embers stoked bright dispel doubts' gorge.
From passions pursued and endless creation spun,
Emanates inspiration – a radiant sun.

Amidst prose poetic, kindled wondrous thought,
Humanity engages deeply, in quests earnestly sought.
In heartening tales, bravery is taught,
Lessons learned, wisdom eagerly bought.

Upon hallowed grounds, visionaries fought,
New worlds are envisioned, worries naught.
Expansive harmony, collectively wrought,
Echoes timeless meaning, each lesson brought.

–

✦✦✦

**HURRY UP PLEASE ITS TIME!**
**HURRY UP PLEASE ITS TIME!**
**HURRY UP PLEASE ITS TIME!**

T. S. Eliot, THE WASTE LAND

---

*Life is a celebration*
*As long as I care for you*
*And you care for me*

Tony Bennett

***

**

*

# Let them not claim

Let there be no claim: we were blind to its unfolding.
We watched.

Let there be no claim: silence was all we offered.
We echoed.

Let them not whisper: our tongues found no taste of its truth.
We consumed, we ached.

Let them not declare: words went unspoken, truths unwritten.
We narrated, our voices and actions stood as testament.

Let them not lament: inertia was their sole response.
Acted we did – yet fell short.

Should they voice an utterance amidst the reckoning;
Call it a phosphorescent tragedy. It smoldered.

Acknowledge then that by its glow did we huddle,
illumined in knowledge bask, and though it razed foundations –
we marveled at its fierce illumination, leaving ashes from which to ask.

Let them not whisper: they were merely spectators to the flame.
We engaged, yet our efforts bore the weight of tomorrow's shade.

Let there be no claim: apathy was their doctrine, their creed.
We cared deeply, our hearts entwined with Earth's every plea.

Let them not insinuate: that in fear, we turned away.
We stood defiant amid storms our own hands helped convey.

Should history seek a label for this epoch carved by fire;
Name it an era where human touch ignited globe entire,

And so they might say amidst ruins or rebirth found;

Within its incandescence did we finally find hallowed ground,

For beneath its fierce illumination — a revelation:
that from embers can spring forth a verdant salvation.

—

This piece is a variation inspired by the powerful themes addressed in "Let Them Not Say" by poet Jane Hirshfield. It seeks to echo and expand upon her reflections on action, awareness, and responsibility within the context of our present Anthropocene era.

~~~

# Manifesto

## A Poet's Manifesto for the Earth – 7.4, 21:22

We, the scribes of the whispering winds and the roaring seas, hereby declare our unwavering commitment to the only home we have ever known: Earth. Bearing the weight of our pens and the power of our words, we pledge to stand as guardians of truth, advocates for justice, and heralds of a future we dare to imagine. In this manifesto, we assert our roles and responsibilities in shaping the dialogue around humanity's relationship with the environment.

### – Articulate the Beauty and the Wounds

We vow to capture both the breathtaking beauty of our planet and the scars we have inflicted upon it. Through vivid imagery and compelling narratives, we will make the invisible visible, and the silent audible. The melting glaciers, the burning forests, and the plastic-choked oceans will find a voice in our verses.

### – Amplify the Marginalised

We commit to lending our voices to those less heard. Recognizing that environmental destruction disproportionately affects the world's most vulnerable populations, we will use our poetry to shine a light on these injustices, ensuring their stories are told and not forgotten.

### – Celebrate Interconnectedness

In every line and stanza, we will champion the truth of our interconnectedness – with each other and with the web of life that sustains us. Our poetry will remind humanity that we are but one thread in the intricate tapestry of existence, urging a collective shift from exploitation to stewardship.

### – Challenge the Status Quo

With words sharp as knives, we will cut through denial and apathy, exposing the folly of unsustainable consumption and the greed that fuels it. Our verses will confront and challenge, demanding accountability from those who put profit above the planet and future generations.

## – Inspire Action and Hope

Yet, in the face of despair, our poetry will be a beacon of hope and a call to action. We will craft visions of a sustainable future, celebrating every act of courage, every step towards conservation, and every success in the restoration of our world. Our words will rally spirits and motivate action, for the pen, wielded with purpose, can be mightier than the sword.

## – Advocate for the Earth

Above all, we pledge to use our poetry as a form of advocacy – a clarion call for the protection and preservation of our environment. Our manifestos, sonnets, and free verse poems will champion the causes of sustainability, conservation, and respect for all life.

In solidarity, we, the poets, unite under the banner of this manifesto. With the Earth as our muse and guide, we commit to this sacred duty, channeling the power of poetry to effect real and lasting change. Let our words be the seeds of a healthier, more harmonious relationship with the planet – a legacy of love and respect for the Earth that sustains us all.

# Notes

## Geologists Say It's Not Time to Declare a Human-Created Epoch. 5.3.2024[1]

A panel of experts voted down a proposal to officially declare the start of a new interval of geologic time, one defined by humanity's changes to the planet.

Is it time to mark humankind's transformation of the planet with its own chapter in Earth history, the "Anthropocene," or the human age?

Not yet, scientists have decided, after a debate that has spanned nearly 15 years. Or the blink of an eye, depending on how you look at it.

In March 2024, after 15 years of deliberation, the Anthropocene Epoch proposal of the AWG was voted down by a wide margin by the SQS, owing largely to its shallow sedimentary record and extremely recent proposed start date. The ICS and the International Union of Geological Sciences (IUGS) later formally confirmed, by a near unanimous vote, the rejection of the AWG's Anthropocene Epoch proposal for inclusion in the Geologic Time Scale. The IUGS statement on the rejection concluded: "Despite its rejection as a formal unit of the Geologic Time Scale, Anthropocene will nevertheless continue to be used not only by Earth and environmental scientists, but also by social scientists, politicians and economists, as well as by the public at large. It will remain an invaluable descriptor of human impact on the Earth system."[2]

By geologists' current timeline of Earth's 4.6-billion-year history, our world right now is in the Holocene, which began 11,700 years ago with the most recent retreat of the great glaciers. Amending the chronology to say we had moved on to the Anthropocene would represent an acknowledgment that recent, human-induced changes to geological conditions had been profound enough to bring the Holocene to a close.

---

1   https://www.nytimes.com/2024/03/05/climate/anthropocene-epoch-vote-rejected.html
2   https://en.wikipedia.org/wiki/Anthropocene

The declaration would shape terminology in textbooks, research articles and museums worldwide. It would guide scientists in their understanding of our still-unfolding present for generations, perhaps even millenniums, to come.

In the end, though, the members of the committee that voted on the Anthropocene over the past month were not only weighing how consequential this period had been for the planet. They also had to consider when, precisely, it began.

By the definition that an earlier panel of experts spent nearly a decade and a half debating and crafting, the Anthropocene started in the mid-20th century, when nuclear bomb tests scattered radioactive fallout across our world. To several members of the scientific committee that considered the panel's proposal in recent weeks, this definition was too limited, too awkwardly recent, to be a fitting signpost of Homo sapiens's reshaping of planet Earth.

"It constrains, it confines, it narrows down the whole importance of the Anthropocene," said Jan A. Piotrowski, a committee member and geologist at Aarhus University in Denmark. "What was going on during the onset of agriculture? How about the Industrial Revolution? How about the colonizing of the Americas, of Australia?"

"Human impact goes much deeper into geological time," said another committee member, Mike Walker, an Earth scientist and professor emeritus at the University of Wales Trinity Saint David. "If we ignore that, we are ignoring the true impact, the real impact, that humans have on our planet."

The grandly named chapters of our planet's history are governed by a body of scientists, the International Union of Geological Sciences. The organization uses rigorous criteria to decide when each chapter started and which characteristics defined it. The aim is to uphold common global standards for expressing the planet's history.

~ ~ ~

# Symbiocene

The term "Symbiocene" is a conceptual idea proposed as an aspirational period following the Anthropocene. Coined by Australian environmental philosopher Glenn Albrecht in 2012, it embodies an era characterised by living in harmony and mutual benefit among humans, other species, and the environment. Unlike the Anthropocene, which highlights human impact on Earth in ways that often reflect damage and imbalance (such as pollution and climate change), the Symbiocene suggests a future where human actions foster ecological health, enrich biodiversity, and restore ecosystems.

In essence, the Symbiocene represents an ideal state of symbiosis or cooperative living where all life forms thrive together through mutual support and sustainable practices. It's envisioned as a shift away from behaviours leading to ecological degradation towards those promoting coexistence and shared prosperity with nature.

~~~

## The "poems" – 9.4, 16:40

As an AI developed by OpenAI, I don't browse the internet or access live databases to retrieve information or content such as poems. Instead, I generate responses based on a mixture of licensed data, data created by human trainers, and publicly available data. The texts and creative pieces like poems that I provide are original creations produced in response to your prompts, drawing upon the vast amount of language patterns and structures I've been trained on.

The "poems" you see in our conversation were not found but generated spontaneously in response to your requests. They're unique compositions intended to match the style or theme you're interested in discussing or exploring further.

~~~

# Resources

Art of the Anthropocene:
https://scalar.usc.edu/works/engl205-05h-fall-2017/index

Rosi Braidotti (2020). "Posthuman knowledge". Polity Press

The Gaia Hypothesis: https://en.wikipedia.org/wiki/Gaia_hypothesis

Locus amoenus, a pleasant place: https://en.wikipedia.org/wiki/Locus_amoenus

# Poets for the Symbiocene

Creating a list of poets who write about the Symbiocene, an era focused on living harmoniously with nature and each other, involves identifying those whose work embodies themes of mutualism, ecology, sustainability, and coexistence. Since the concept is relatively new and specific poetry collections might not explicitly label themselves as "Symbiocene" poetry, we look for poets whose work resonates with these themes. Here's a hypothetical compilation that aligns well with these ideals:

1. **Gary Snyder** - A poet deeply rooted in environmentalism and Zen Buddhism, his poetry often reflects a profound connection to nature and advocates for ecological balance.

2. **Wendell Berry** - His work eloquently speaks to the importance of community, sustainable farming practices, and the deep bond between humans and Earth.

3. **Camille T. Dungy** - Editor of "Black Nature: Four Centuries of African American Nature Poetry," Dungy's own poetry frequently explores racial narratives within natural settings while celebrating resilience in both human and non-human contexts.

4. **Mary Oliver** - Renowned for her clear-eyed observations of the natural world, Mary Oliver may no longer be with us, yet her legacy endures. Her work continues to inspire love and respect for ecosystems through its keen observations and detailed lyricism. Oliver's grounding ethos underscores the urgent need to protect and cherish our surroundings.

5. **Robin Wall Kimmerer** - Although more widely known as a scientist (botanist) and author of "Braiding Sweetgrass," her narrative style blends indigenous wisdom and scientific knowledge into a poetic appreciation of plants and the symbiotic relationships they entail.

6. **Craig Santos Perez** - As a Chamorro poet from Guam, he brings attention to issues of colonialism and climate change and their impact on island ecosystems and communities, intertwining personal and collective histories to broaden understanding of the interconnections that sustain human and non-human worlds alike.

7. **Joy Harjo** - Poet Laureate of the United States and of Native American heritage, her works imbue spirituality and explore ways in which culture, tradition, and eco-consciousness fuse, restraining forces of destruction and fostering flourishing art equally as celebration, lament, and reminder of ancestry's obligation to stewardship for future generations.

8. **John Powell** - Not traditionally classified as a "poet," nonetheless his writings on equitable society and inclusive embrace of humanity's variances strike a chord echoing principles extending beyond mere acknowledgment of diversity. His works seek to engage in dialogue through truly regenerative, holistic frameworks that envision prospects unifying disparate elements into a wholeness embracing both difference and strength, underscoring interconnected well-being.

Including these poets offers readers various lenses through which to view and envision concepts central to the emergence of thoughtful reflections inherent in literature. Their profound contributions encourage active participation in the evolving story where the embodiment of symbiotic philosophy is realised through imaginative and explorative means. Every voice on this list contributes to a tapestry of meanings, colours, and fabric that we hope will represent a diverse, empathetic, and reflective movement towards the Symbiocene.

*Today I may not have a thing at all*
*Except for just a dream or two*
*But I've got lots of plans for tomorrow*
*And all my tomorrows belong to you*

Alexander Thoma

Scriptum anno
MMXXIV
de Anthropocene
per ChatGPT